Spanish

The Effective Beginners Guide for Spanish

Table of Contents

Introduction

This book contains proven steps and strategies on how you can learn to converse in Spanish. We start with the building blocks of the language into more complex subjects like grammar. This book is designed especially for beginners who are eager to learn about the language. The lessons are easy to follow and they come with plenty of examples to facilitate a more effective learning.

But you may be wondering "why the need to educate yourself on this foreign language?" What's in it for you?

Spanish is among the most common languages spoken by people all over the world. In fact, it is the second most commonly spoken in the United States. Spanish is the language of romantics.

History of Spanish

We know Spanish as a romantic language. There's something about the way the string of words sound like. It is as if it is meant to woo a lover.

This is why you may be surprised to know that Spanish is actually derived from Vulgar Latin, the kind of Latin spoken by Roman soldiers. By 200 BC, this form of Latin became more popular and widespread throughout the Empire. And Vulgar Latin gave birth to Spanish and other romantic languages that we know today - Italian, French, Romanian and Portuguese.

Because Spanish shares a lot with these languages, it is quite easy to learn the others once you have a good understanding of the Spanish language and vice versa.

Benefits of Learning Spanish

It is easy to stick with your native tongue. As an English speaker, you may feel like you have a huge advantage. After all, English is supposed to be the universal language, correct? But have you not ever been fascinated by other languages, by other cultures? Do you not find them fascinating?

Learning Spanish, or a new language for that matter, gives you an opportunity to learn things beyond your comfort zone, to explore outside the world you were born into and to have a better appreciation of people and other culture.

It Will Make It Easier to Travel

Nobody really likes being treated like a typical ""tourist." For one, you will spend more being the "ignorant" traveler that you are desperately trying to communicate with locals in English or rummaging through words in your Spanish dictionary. On the other hand, speaking the local language gives you more freedom. You can immediately build rapport with the locals. You are less likely to get lost as you can ask for directions from anyone. And you can get better prices when you go shopping.

It Makes Meeting Other People Easier

Knowing the language makes you more approachable. Remember, when you travel to Spain, you are the foreigner. English is their foreign language. You simply cannot expect everyone to know your native language. It translates to arrogance. A foreigner in Spain speaking Spanish creates quite an impression. The fastest way to please locals and encourage them to open up is showing an effort to get to know them and it starts with speaking their language.

This does not only apply to traveling. In your social life or career, you are bound to meet people from other countries. And these people may speak English too, which is good as it makes conversing effortless. But you can make a much better impression knowing another language, especially if it is the other person's native tongue. You make them feel at home. And that gives you the opportunity to make a connection. You can use this advantage to build your network.

It Makes Learning and Exploration Much More Fun

You can probably learn much about a certain culture from reading history books. The beauty of exploring, however, goes beyond that. It is much more fun and fascinating learning a culture from a local's perspective. This way, it becomes a personal experience.

Finally, you should never stop learning! Scientific studies report that learning a new language does something to your brain. It encourages neuroplasticity. It makes you sharper!

Thanks again for downloading this book, I hope you enjoy it!

Chapter 1 - Fast Track Spanish

Before we go into the basics, the pronunciation and grammar rules, I thought you should know a few shortcuts to learning Spanish instantly. This is not to take away the importance of learning the basics. In fact, these shortcuts can enhance your learning process.

Convert English Words to Spanish

Did you know that English and Spanish have a lot of words in common? They are not exactly the same but they can sound alike and share the same meaning. Some English words trace their roots from Latin. They are referred to as Cognates.

Among the most identifiable Cognates are the English words ending in **-TY**. You can easily translate these words to Spanish by replacing the ending with **-DAD**. Here are a few examples.

University - *Universidad*

Velocity - *Velocidad*

Eternity - *Eternidad*

Humanity - *Humanidad*

Can you come up with more English words ending in -TY?

Use Mnemonics

From Cognates to mnemonics, you can use this trick for learning Spanish or any foreign language. All you need to do is find a connection between your mother tongue and the one you're trying to learn. Making an association between words allows you to access your right brain, the creative side. And this makes remembering and learning much faster.

Here's a simple one. The Spanish term for bread is pan. How do you make the connection? Don't you put bread in a pan? Get it now? Mnemonics are more effective when you make the association more personal.

Start with Power Words

You cannot expect to learn all Spanish words. Most of them you will learn as you encounter them. To be able to converse properly, all you need is a hundred words. It applies to Spanish and all other languages. Focus on learning basic words. What are the most commonly used words?

Combine Power Words with Power Verbs

Along with power words, there are most commonly used verbs. Apply cognate rules and mnemonics to remember them easily. If you combine the power words with the power verbs, you can easily create simple sentences in Spanish.

Translate Your Expressions

You probably have a list of phrases and sentences that you use in casual conversations. Why don't you try looking for their translation in Spanish?

In the same way, there may be Spanish expressions that you can use in your everyday conversation. Use them instead. As you use them more often, you start to learn them by heart. You'll make yourself proud and that is great motivation for learning more! And before you know it, you're on your way to mastering the language.

Chapter 2 – Letters and Numbers

Now you know a few tricks that can help fast track your learning. So, let's go to the basics. One of the first things you need to familiarize yourself with when learning a new language is the alphabet. In Spanish, the alphabet is referred to as **abecedario**. It has 27 letters. Along with the letters, a guide for pronunciation is provided which is how the letters should sound like when you recite them.

A	pronounced as	AH
B	pronounced as	BEH
Che	pronounced as	CHE
C	pronounced as	CE
D	pronounced as	DE
E	pronounced as	E
F	pronounced as	EFE
G	pronounced as	GE
H	pronounced as	HACHE
I	pronounced as	I
J	pronounced as	JOTA
K	pronounced as	KA
L	pronounced as	ELE
Ll	pronounced as	ELLE

M	pronounced as	EME
N	pronounced as	ENE
Ñ	pronounced as	EÑE
O	pronounced as	O
P	pronounced as	PE
Q	pronounced as	CU
R	pronounced as	ERE
RR	pronounced as	ERRE
S	pronounced as	ESE
T	pronounced as	TE
U	pronounced as	U
V	pronounced as	VE
W	pronounced as	DOBLE UVE
X	pronounced as	EQUIS
Y	pronounced as	I GRIEGA
Z	pronounced as	ZETA

Spanish Pronunciation Guide

These letters make a different sound however when they are used in words. For instance, Ll makes an EY-YEY sound and H is always silent. Here are a few sample words for each letter and how they are pronounced properly.

LETTER	PRONUNCIATION	EXAMPLE	TRANSLATION
A	Like in "fAther"	*Amigo* (a-mee-go)	Male friend
B	Like in "Ball"	*Bonita* (bo-nee-ta)	Pretty
CHE	Like in "CHair"	*Chaqueta* (cha-ke-ta)	Jacket
C	Soft C like in "Cell" Hard C like in "Call"	*Cielo* (sye-lo) *Camiseta* (ka-mee-se-ta)	Sky Shirt
D	Like in "Daddy"	*Dedo* (de-do)	Finger
E	Like in "Egg"	*Español* (es-pa-nyol)	Spanish
F	Like in "Fun"	*Final* (fee-nal)	End or Finish
G	Soft G like in H in "Hello" Hard G like in "Go"	*Genial* (he-nyal) *Graso/ Grasa* (gra-so/	Great Fatty or Greasy

		gra-sa)	
H	Silent	*Hambre* (am-bre)	Hunger
I	EE like in "see"	*Idea* (ee-de-ya)	Idea
J	Like in "House"	*Jardin* (har-deen)	Garden
K	Like in "Kite"	*Ketchup* (ket-choop)	Ketchup
L	Like in "Like"	*Lobo* (lo-bo)	Wolf
LL	Like Y in "Yell"	*cabaLLero* (ka-ba-ye-ro)	Gentleman
M	Like in "Mother"	*Madre* (mad-re)	Mother
N	Like in "Next"	*Negro* (neg-ro)	Black
Ñ	NY like in "caNYon"	*EspaÑol* (es-pa-nyol)	Spanish
O	Like in "rOll"	*Ojo* (o-ho)	Eye
P	Like in ""Peanut"	*Poco* (po-ko)	Little or Small
Q	K like in "Keep"	*Quiza* (kwi-za)	Maybe
R	Like in "Ring"	*cueRpo*	Body

		(kwer-po)	
RR	Trilled sound like in "Brr"	*peRRo* (per-ro)	Dog
S	Like in "Sad"	**S***alud* (sa-lood)	Health
T	Like in "Tax"	*Tamaño* (ta-ma-nyo)	Size
U	OO like in "root"	*mUndo* (moon-do)	World
V	Like the soft B sound in "cupBoard"	*Vacacion* (ba-ka-syon)	Vacation
W	Like in "Whiskey"	Wafle (waf-le)	Waffle
X	H sound like in "Hello"	México (me-hee-ko)	Mexico
Y	Like in "yes"	*Yate* (ya-te)	Yacht
Z	Like in "zipper"	*Zapato* (za-pa-to)	Shoe

You may have noticed in the above examples that Spanish vowels take on one sound. There's only one way to pronounce them unlike in English where the vowel sounds have variations. Spanish A for instance, is just Ah whereas English A can either be short or long.

Now, you may be wondering when you should use a soft C, soft G and a hard C or G. In most cases, hard C applies. In cases when the letter appears before the vowels I or E however, C takes on an S sound rather than a K sound. Spanish letter G takes on a similar sound as in English especially when it appears after L, M, N or after a pause. When it is used before vowels E or I however, it takes on a harsh H sound like how you would pronounce Spanish J.

If you want to practice your pronunciation, the best way to do it is to keep reading Spanish words. You can also refer to a Spanish-English dictionary. This way, you have a clear reference on proper pronunciation. And do not forget to speak the words out loud. This is way better than mental reading. Not only can you hear yourself make the sound, you also get to feel how each sound feels in your lips and tongue.

Días de la Semana (Days of the Week)

It's time to learn more Spanish words. You can try using these words to tell someone about your day or how you spend your weekend. Use them as often as you can. Write them on your planner. Use them in creating your to-do list.

Domingo	(do-meeng-go)	~	Sunday
Lunes	(loo-nes)	~	Monday
Martes	(mar-tes)	~	Tuesday
Miercoles	(mi-yer-ko-les)	~	Wednesday
Jueves	(hwe-bes)	~	Thursday
Viernes	(byer-nes)	~	Friday
Sabado	(sa-ba-do)	~	Saturday

Remember to use the soft B sound for the V in *Jueves* and *Viernes* like the B in "cupboard."

Meses y Tiempos (Months and Seasons)

From days to months, you should find these words easy enough to memorize.

enero	(e-ne-ro)	~ January
febrero	(feb-re-ro)	~ February

marzo	(mar-zo)	~ March
abril	(a-breel)	~ April
mayo	(ma-yo)	~ May
junio	(hoo-nyo)	~ June
julio	(hool-yo)	~ July
ogosto	(o-gos-to)	~ August
septiembre	(sep-tyem-bre)	~ September
octubre	(ok-toob-re)	~ October
noviembre	(no-byem-bre)	~ November
diciembre	(dee-syem-bre)	~ December
primavera	(pree-ma-be-ra)	~ Spring
verano	(be-ra-no)	~ Summer
otoño	(o-ton-yo)	~ Fall
invierno	(een-byer-no)	~ Winter

Números (Numbers)

After learning the abecederos, it's time you learn to count in Spanish. Learn them by heart by replacing your English numbers with their Spanish counterpart. Let's begin with numbers 1 to 31.

1 – *Uno*   (oo-no)

2 – *Dos*   (dos)

3 – *Tres*   (tres)

4 – *Cuatro*   (kwat-ro)

5 – *Cinco*   (seeng-ko)

6 – *Seis*   (se-ees)

7 – *Siete*   (sye-te)

8 – *Ocho*   (o-cho)

9 – *Nueve*   (new-be)

10 – *Diez*   (dyez)

11 – *Once*   (on-se)

12 – *Doce*   (do-se)

13 – *Trece*   (tre-se)

14 – *Catorce*   (ka-tor-se)

15 – *Quince*   (keen-se)

16 – *Dieciseis*   (dee-see-se-ees)

17 – *Diecisiete*   (dee-see-sye-te)

18 – *Dieciocho*   (dee-see-o-cho)

19 – *Diecinueve* (dee-see-new-be)

20 - *Veinte*   (beyn-te)

21 - *Veintiuno*   (beyn-tee-oo-no)

22 - *Veintidos*   (beyn-tee-dos)

23 - *Veintitres*   (beyn-tee-tres)

24 - *Veinticuatro* (beyn-tee-kwat-ro)

25 - *Veinticinco* (beyn-tee-seeng-ko)

26 - *Veintiseis*   (beyn-tee-se-ees)

27 - *Veintisiete* (beyn-tee-sye-te)

28 - *Veintiocho*   (beyn-tee-o-cho)

29 - *Veintinueve* (beyn-tee-new-be)

30 - *Treinta*   (treyn-ta)

31 - *Treinta y uno*   (treyn-tay-oo-noo)

From 31 onwards, we use the Spanish *y* which means "and." This means 32 = 30 and 2. *Y* is pronounced as EY. If it follows a vowel, the sound should continue with the vowel sound. This is why 31 is pronounced as (treyn-tay-oo-noo) instead of (treyn-ta e oo-noo).

40 - *Cuarenta*   (kwa-ren- ta)

50 – *Cincuenta*   (seeng-kwen-ta)

60 – *Sesenta*   (se-sen-ta)

70 – *Setenta*   (se-ten-ta)

80 – *Ochenta*   (o-chen-ta)

90 – *Noventa*   (no-ben-ta)

100 - *Cien*   (syen)

1000 – *Mil*   (meel)

Now here are a few challenges. Can you say how old you are in Spanish? What is your house number? Can you recite your phone number in Spanish?

Decir la Hora (Telling Time)

Let's get into more specifics. Using your newly learned Spanish numbers, you can now start learning how to tell the time using the language.

The question is "*¿Qué hora es?*" which is translated to English as "What time is it?" How do you answer it? You can use this formula.

Son las + the hour

Son las dos.   ~ It is 2:00.

Son las diez.   ~ It is 10:00.

Son las tres.   ~ It is 3:00.

Es la una. ~ It is 1:00.

Did you notice that the last example does not exactly follow the format? That's because it's **una** or 1 and it cannot be plural. **Es** is the singular form of **Son** in the same way as **la** is the singular form of **las**.

Telling the time in Spanish is easy, right? The thing is it won't be exactly 2:00 all the time. How do you tell the exact time up to the last minute? All you need to do is add **y** which means "and" then you can continue with the number of minutes.

For "quarter", use the Spanish word **cuarto**. For "fifteen", you can use the Spanish word **quince**. These two will be useful if you want to say "It is 15 minutes past 3:00" instead of saying "It is 3:15." Instead of using **treinta** for 30 minutes, you can also use **media** which means "half".

Son las dos y dieciséis.   ~ It is 2:16.

Son las diez y treinta y uno. ~ It is 10:31.

Son las tres y veintitres.   ~ It is 3:23.

Es la una y cincuenta y seis. ~ It is 1:56.

Son las doce y cuarto.   ~ It is 12:15.

Son las doce y quince.	~ It is 12:15.
Son las once y treinta.	~ It is 11:30.
Son las once y media.	~ It is 11:30.

How do you say "It is 1:50" differently? You can say "It is ten to 2:00." How do you say this in Spanish? You can use the word **menos**. ***Son las dos menos diez.***

The Spanish uses a 24-hour clock. This means 1:00 pm is 13:00. Alternatively, you can use 12 hour clock but you need to add a few words. Use the following format.

Son las + the time + *de la mañana* (in the morning)

Es la + the time + *de la tarde* (in the afternoon)

Son las + the time + *de la noche* (in the evening)

Instead of saying 12:00 in the afternoon, you can simply say "noon." Instead of saying 12:00 at night, you can simply say "midnight." This is how you say it in Spanish.

Es medianoche. ~ It is midnight.

Es mediodía.   ~ It is noon.

With regard to time, there are two important questions. These are **"a qué hora"** "what" or "at what time" and **"cuándo"** or "when" For instance, you may be asked the following and this is how you can answer.

¿Cuándo vamos al centro comercial?   ~ When are we going to the mall?

Vamos al centro comercial a la mediodia. ~ We are going to the mall at noon.

¿A qué hora llamada Maria?   ~ At what time does Maria call?

Maria llama a las dos de la semana.   ~ Maria calls at 2:00 AM.

You can also talk about events that happened in the past in a certain time. The past tense of the Spanish word **estar** should be used which are **eran** (plural) and **era** (singular).

Era la una de la semana.   ~ It was 1:00 in the morning.

Eran las tres de la tarde.   ~ It was 3:00 in the afternoon.

In the same way, you can talk about the future. For instance, you can express what is about to happen in 30 minutes or in 4 hours using the following phrases.

En treinta minutos...   ~ In 30 minutes...

En cuatro horas...   ~ In 4 hours...

Indicando la Fecha (Telling the Date)

Telling the time of the day is simply not enough. You also need to learn to talk about events as they relate to specific dates. Unlike in English, the Spanish date is written or stated with the day first followed by the month and year.

5 de febrero de 1985 or 05/02/1985   ~   February 5, 1985 or 02/05/1985

16 de julio de 2001   or 16/07/2001   ~   July 16, 2001 or 07/16/2001

25 de diciembre de 2016 or 25/12/2016 ~ December 25, 2016 or 12/25/2016

So this is the standard format when expressing date in Spanish:

el + **day** + **de** + **month** + **de** + **year**

There is one exception you should take note of. When talking about the first day of the month, you should say **el primero** instead of **el uno**. Here's an example: **el primero de enero de 1996** (January 1, 1996).

Now let's talk about the year. In English, we read dates in two's. So we read 1996 as nineteen ninety six. In Spanish, it is read as one thousand nine hundred ninety six.

1984 - *Mil novecientos ochenta y cuatro*

2001 - *Dos mil uno*

2016 - *Dos mil dieciséis*

If you want to talk about an event happening in the future without a specific day, you can use the Spanish preposition **en** which is the equivalent to the English preposition "in". On the other hand, if there is a specific date to the event, you should use the Spanish preposition **el** whose English equivalent is "on".

La fiesta será en julio.   ~ The party will be in July.

La fiesta será el cuatro de julio.   ~ The party will be on July 4.

Saludos Despedidas (Greetings)

Every good conversation starts with greetings. Proper greetings can help you make a good impression. You have time to learn grammar rules in the succeeding chapters. For now, let us proceed with basic Spanish greetings.

Hola	~ Hello
Buenos días	~ Good morning
Buenas tardes	~ Good afternoon
Buenas noches	~ Good evening or goodnight
Por favor	~ Please
Gracias	~ Thank you
De nada	~ Welcome
Adios	~ Goodbye
Hasta luego	~ Until later

If you want to know someone's name, you simply ask **"¿Cómo te llamas?"** Now there are different ways to respond to this question. Use the following as reference.

Mi nombre es ... ~ My name is...

Me llamo... ~ I am called...

Yo soy... ~ I am...

After the introduction, you can use the following phrases too.

Encantado mucho gusto. (masculine) ~ Nice to meet you.

Encantada mucho gusto. (feminine) ~ Nice to meet you.

El gusto es mío. ~ The pleasure is mine.

Igualmente. ~ The same to you.

You may also want to ask how the other person is doing. There are two ways to ask "How are you" in Spanish. The formal version is "***Como está usted?***" The informal or more casual way of asking is "***Como estas?***" In response to the question, the following phrases may be used.

Muy Bien ~ Very good

Así así/ Regular ~ So-so

Mal ~ Bad

You can start incorporating all that you've learned in this chapter in your daily conversations. It is best that you familiarize yourself fully with all these things first before proceeding to the next lessons.

Chapter 3 - Nouns

In English, nouns can either be plural or singular. In addition to the number of nouns in Spanish, you also have to be mindful of gender. That's right. Spanish nouns cannot only be singular or plural. They also have gender. Some are masculine. Others are feminine. There are a couple of nouns too which may be neutral.

Masculine or Feminine

How do you know if a noun is masculine or feminine? A quick way is to pay attention to the ending. Nouns that end in **L, O, R, E, N, S** are usually masculine. Those ending in **D, A, N, Z, Ción** on the other hand, are typically feminine. Let us look at the following examples.

Masculine		Feminine	
Árbol	Tree	*Juventud*	Youth
Regalo	Gift	*Mancha*	Stain
Plátano	Banana	*Manzana*	Apple
Dormitorio	Bedroom	*Piscina*	Pool
Teatro	Theatre	*Rosa*	Rose
Tío	Uncle	*Profesora*	Professor

Niño	Son/Child	*Enfermera*	Nurse
Cartero	Postman/Mailman	*Canción*	Song
Queso	Cheese	*Iglesia*	Church
Bebé	Baby	*Cosa*	Thing
Examen	Exam	*Circulación*	Traffic

It is easy to jump into conclusions and think that nouns associated with women are feminine and vice versa. When it comes to Spanish nouns, the opposite applies. Let us have a closer look.

Masculine		Feminine	
Salvaseis	Pantyliner	*Guitarra*	Guitar
Paraguas	Umbrella	*Ginebra*	Gin
Maquillaje	Makeup	*Antifaz*	Mask
Pantys	Tights	*Corbata*	Tie
Camisón	Nightdress	*Cantera*	Case

In addition, nouns that end in accented vowels like **á, é, í, ó** and **ú** are also masculine. Most nouns that end in consonants except for those sending in **-d**, **-z** and -

ión are also part of the masculine group. Abstract nouns however, are usually feminine.

Masculine		Feminine	
Colibrí	Humming Bird	*Felicidad*	Happiness
Ají	Chili Pepper	*Paz*	Peace
Cojín	Cushion	*Virtud*	Virtue
Rumor	Rumor	*Salud*	Health

Exceptions:

The word ending rule is not always reliable. It simply does not apply to all nouns. There are a couple of exceptions. In the following list of examples, you may find nouns ending in D, A, N, Z, Ción that may actually be masculine instead of feminine. Similarly, some nouns ending in L, O, R, E, N, S may be feminine rather than masculine.

Since these nouns are rule breakers, you need to memorize them until you know them by heart.

Masculine		Feminine	
Día	Day	*Cárcel*	Prison
Pez	Fish	*Flor*	Flower

Arroz	Rice	*Noche*	Night
Bistec	Steak	*Lente*	Lens
Esquí	Ski	*Razón*	Reason
Reloj	Watch	*Calle*	Street

While most nouns that end in −**A** are feminine, nouns ending in −**MA** can be masculine. In the meantime, some nouns that end in −**E** are feminine. Other Spanish nouns ending in **-pa** and **-ta** with Greek origins are masculine as well.

Masculine Nouns Ending in -MA		Feminine Nouns Ending in −E	
Drama	Drama	*Llave/ Clave*	Key
Enigma	Mystery	*Fiebre*	Fever
Esquema	Scheme	*Carne*	Meat
Estigma	Stigma	*Gente*	People
Estratega	Strategist	*Nieve*	Snow
Idioma	Language	*Nube*	Cloud
Mapa	Map	*Sangre*	Blood
Planeta	Planet	*Suerte*	Luck
Problema	Problem	*Muerte*	Death

Sistema	System	*Clase*	Class
Buda	Buddha	*Corriente*	Current
Carisma	Charisma	*Fuente*	Source
Clima	Weather	*Sede*	Headquarters
Prisma	Prism	*Serpiente*	Snake
Fantasma	Ghost	*Torre*	Tower

Feminine Nouns Ending in –**O**

Foto ~ Photo

Mano ~
Hand

Moto ~
Motorcycle

Libido ~
Libido

Radio ~
Radio

Polio ~ Polio

Femine Nouns ending in -**L** and -**R**

Miel ~ Honey

Sal ~ Salt

Hiel ~ Gall

Piel ~ Skin

Coliflor ~
Cauliflower

Labor ~
Work

Masculine Nouns Ending in -**D**

Huésped	~ Guest	*Áspid*	~ Viper
Césped	~ Grass	*Laúd*	~ Lute
Abad	~ Abbot	*Récord*	~ Record
Alud	~ Avalanche		

Masculine Nouns Ending in -Z

Aprendiz	~ Apprentice	*Altavoz*	~ Speaker
Cáliz	~ Chalice	*Altramuz*	~ Lupins
Ajedrez	~ Chess	*Barniz*	~ Varnish
Maíz	~ Corn	*Cariz*	~ Look
Albornoz	~ Bathrobe	*Disfraz*	~ Costume
Avestruz	~ Ostrich	*Matiz*	~ Hue

So why is it important to learn whether a noun is masculine or feminine? Just like how English verbs need to follow the singularity or plurality of a noun, Spanish verbs, adjectives and articles need to agree not only with the number of the noun but also in gender.

Singular to Plural

The English language has different ways of turning a singular noun to its plural form. It usually involves adding a suffix which depends on how the noun ends. The same is true for Spanish nouns. Here are the basic rules for turning singular Spanish nouns to plural.

1. Add **-s** to nouns ending in vowels

Singular	Plural	Translation
Calle	Calles	Streets
Plaza	Plazas	Towns
Gato	Gatos	Cats
Vaca	Vacas	Cows

2. Add **-es** to nouns that end in consonants

Singular	Plural	Translation
Hotel	Hoteles	Hotels
Ciudad	Ciudades	Cities
Color	Colores	Colors
Papel	Papeles	Papers

3. Singular nouns ending in **S** remain unchanged in their plural form like **Jueves** (Thursday/s).

In some cases however, suffix **−es** must be added to nouns already ending in **S** like *Mes* (month). Its plural form is *Meses* (months).

4. To turn singular nouns ending in **Z** in their plural form, Z must be dropped and replaced with **C** then attach suffix **−es**.

Singular	Plural	Translation
Lápiz	*Lápices*	Pencils
Vez	*Veces*	Number of times
Luz	*Luces*	Lights
Pez	*Peces*	Fishes

Definite versus Indefinite Articles

Indefinite articles do not refer to anything specific. In English, our definite articles are "a" for nouns ending that begin with a consonant and "an" for those that start with a vowel. Definite articles on the other hand, are used to refer to something very specific. There is only one definite article in the English language. It is "the." Articles are pretty simple in English. Their Spanish equivalents are a little more complex. There are a couple of things you need to consider.

First, you must find out whether a definite or indefinite article applies. Second, you need to determine the gender of the noun. In some cases, this can be determined by looking at the letter it ends with. Third, you also need to determine whether it is singular or plural.

<u>Spanish Definite Articles</u>

El ~ if noun is masculine and singular i.e. *el libro* (the book)

La ~ if noun is feminine and singular i.e. *la chica* (the girl)

Los ~ if noun is masculine and plural i.e. *los libros* (the books)

Las ~ if noun is feminine and plural i.e. *las chicas* (the girls)

<u>Spanish Indefinite Articles</u>

Un ~ if noun is masculine and singular i.e. *un libro* (a book)

Una ~ if noun is feminine and singular i.e. *una chica* (a girl)

Unos ~ if noun is masculine and plural i.e. *unos libros* (a few books/ some books)

Unas ~ if noun is feminine and plural i.e. *unas chicas* (a few girls/ some girls)

VOCABULARY

Let us enrich your Spanish vocabulary further. Pay attention as you will find most of these nouns useful.

Partes del Cuerpo (Parts of the Body)

el dedo del pie	~ toe	el oreja	~ ear
el pie	~ foot	el pelo	~ hair
el dedo	~ finger	el cerebro	~ brain
el codo	~ elbow	la perna	~ leg
el brazo	~ arm	la muñeca	~ wrist
el corazón	~ heart	la espalda	~ back
el estómigo	~ stomach	la cintura	~ waist
el pecho	~ chest	la naríz	~ nose
el hombro	~ shoulder	la boca	~ mouth
el cuello	~ neck	la cara	~ face
el ojo	~ eye	la cabeza	~ head

Piezas de Ropa (Pieces of Clothing)

el anillo	~ ring	el traje de bañar	~ swimsuit
el vestido	~ dress		
el sombrero	~ hat	los guantes	~ gloves

los zapatos ~ shoes

los calcetines ~ socks

los pantelones ~ pants

los pendientes ~ earrings

la capa ~ coat

la correa ~ belt

la falda ~ skirt

la blusa ~ blouse

la camisa ~ shirt

La Casa (House)

el baño ~ bathroom

el cuarto ~ room

el vestíbulo ~ hallway

cuarto de cenar ~ dining room

la pared ~ wall

la ventana ~ window

la pila ~ sink

la cocina ~ kitchen

la sala ~ living room

ducha ~ shower

bañera ~ bathtub

apartamento ~ apartment

armario ~ closet

azotea ~ roof

escaleras ~ stairs

Muebles (Furniture)

el horno ~ oven

el puerto ~ door

la basura ~ garbage

la refrijedora ~ refrigerator

la luz ~ light

la silla ~ chair

la mesa ~ table

microonda ~ microwave

estufa ~ stove

televisión ~ television

manta ~ blanket

cama ~ bed

lavaplatos ~ dishwasher

escritorio ~ desk

sofá ~ couch

Lugares (Places)

el estadio ~ stadium

el restaurante ~ restaurant

el parque ~ park

el museo ~ museum

el cine ~ movie theater

el mercado ~ market

el hogar ~ home

el gardín ~ garden

el café ~ cafe

el banco ~ bank

el aeropuerto ~ airport

la escuela ~ school

la piscina ~ pool

la farmácia ~ pharmacy

la biblioteca ~ library

la hospital ~ hospital

la fábrica ~ factory

la iglesia ~ church

la playa ~ beach

parque zoológico ~ zoo

librería ~ bookstore

tienda ~ store

panaderia ~ pastry shop

almacén ~ grocery store

lapanadería ~ bakery

la estación del tren ~ train station

la estación de la policía ~ police station

Transporte (Transportation)

en tren ~ by train

en taxi ~ by taxi

en subterráneo ~ by subway

en motocicleta ~ by motorcycle

en ciclomotor ~ by moped

a pie ~ on foot

en automovíl ~ by car

en bus ~ by bus

en barco ~ by boat

en bicicleta ~ by bicycle

en avión ~ by airplane

los direcciones ~ directions

Negocio (Business)

la información ~ information

la estimación ~ estimate

el salido ~ exit

la cuenta ~ bill

la entrada ~ entrance

el précio ~ price

las aduanas ~ customs

la cuesta ~ the cost

el impuesto ~ tax

el equipaje ~ luggage/baggage

la renta ~ the rent

el passaporte ~ passport

la officina ~ office

la ciudad ~ city

el cheque ~ check

el cheque de viajar ~ travelers check

el intercambio de modernidad ~ currency exchange

Escuela (School)

el lapicero ~ pen

la computadora ~ computer

el lapiz ~ pencil

maestro/maestra ~ teacher

el papel ~ paper

el diccionário ~ dictionary

estudiente ~ student

el colegio ~ college

profesor/a ~ professor

idiomas extranjeros ~ foreign languages

Naturaleza (Nature)

el relámpago ~ lightning

el campo ~ field/meadow

el granizo ~ hail

el nieve ~ snow

el cielo ~ sky

el arco iris ~ rainbow

el lago ~ lake

el río ~ river

el océano ~ ocean

el bosque ~ forest

los árboles ~ trees

la niebla ~ fog

la lluvia ~ rain

la montaña ~ mountain

la colina ~ hill

la charca ~ pond

niebla ~ cloud

cascada ~ waterfall

selva ~ jungle

planta ~ plant

Animales (Animals)

el mono ~ monkey

el elefante ~ elephant

el lobo ~ wolf

el oso ~ bear

el tigre ~ tiger

el lión ~ lion

el caballo ~ horse

la ballena ~ whale

la mofeta ~ skunk

la cabra ~ goat

la vaca ~ cow

águila ~ eagle

oveja sheep	~	*ratón* mouse	~
cerdo/a	~ pig	*gato/a*	~ cat
pato/a	~ duck	*perro/a*	~ dog
ave	~ bird	*gallina/gallo* ~ chicken/rooster	

Surely, it will take you time to master these nouns. You do not necessarily have to memorize them. However, you are strongly encouraged to read through them over and over and at the same time, make an effort to use them in daily conversations. Practice makes perfect!

Chapter 4 – Pronouns and Adjectives

A substitute of nouns, a pronoun makes it easier to formulate sentences. It also helps you avoid redundancies. In Spanish, there are different types of pronouns just like there are in English. For the purpose of this book, we will be focusing on subjective and objective pronouns.

Subject Pronouns

The English language has I, he/she/it, you, we, and they. And while subject pronouns may be used over and over in English, the same cannot be said for Spanish subject pronouns. Why is that? It is because Spanish verbs are conjugated according to the subject. Indicating the subject pronoun will be redundant. Besides, you should be able to tell the subject based on the way the verb is conjugated.

So in subject pronouns, there are 3 persons: first person, second person and third person. And there are singular and plural forms. In addition, there are formal and informal terms to be learned in Spanish. Please refer to the table below.

	Singular	Plural
1st Person	*Yo* (I)	*Nosotros* (We)

2nd Person **Informal**	*Tu* (You)	*Vosotros* (You all)
Formal	*Usted*	*Ustedes*
3rd Person **Male**	*El* (he)	*Ellos* (they)
Female	*Ella* (she)	*Ellas* (they)

Direct Object Pronouns

In English, we know direct objects as the ones that appear after the verb. We identify them by asking two important questions "whom" or "what" the verb is exactly acting upon. Let's look at these examples.

The girls threw <u>Jorge</u> into the pool.   Whom did the girls throw?

Maria brought <u>food</u> to the party.   What did Maria bring?

Now these objects: "Jorge" and "food" can be replaced by pronouns which are referred to as direct object pronouns. In which case, "Jorge" is replaced by "him" and "food" is replaced by it. The table below shows you Spanish direct object pronouns.

	Singular	**Plural**
1st Person		

	Me (me)	*Nos* (us)
2nd Person **Informal**	*Te* (You)	*Os* (You all)
Formal	*Lo, La*	*Lo, Las*
3rd Person **Male**	*Lo* (him, it)	*Los* (them)
Female	*La* (her, it)	*Las* (them)

The same basic rules apply when using these Spanish pronouns. One, they must agree with the object they are replacing, the number and the gender. In Spanish however, these direct object pronouns usually come before the verb. There are exceptions but for this time, let us stick with the basics.

(Subject) + Direct Object Pronoun + Verb

*Ellas **lo** lanzaron a la piscina.* ~ The girls threw <u>him</u> into the pool.

*Ella **lo** llevó a la fiesta.* ~She brought <u>it</u> to the party.

Indirect Object Pronouns

In contrast to direct objects, indirect objects are the recipient of the action or the verb. To identify the

49

indirect object in a sentence, the questions to ask are either "for whom" or "to whom?"

They gave the food <u>to us</u>.   The food was given to whom?

She works hard <u>for her child</u>.   She works hard for whom?

In the examples above, the indirect object in the second sentence will be replaced by the indirect object pronoun "him." The table below shows you the Spanish indirect object pronouns.

	Singular	**Plural**
1st Person	*Me* (me)	*Nos* (us)
2nd Person **Informal** **Formal**	*Te* (You) *Le*	*Os* (You all) *Les*
3rd Person **Male/Female**	*Le* (him, her, it)	*Les* (them)

Spanish indirect object pronouns also usually appear before the verb.

(Subject) + Indirect Object Pronoun + Verb

*Ella **nos** leí el libro.* ~ She
reads the book to us.

*Nosotros **les** dio el teléfono.* ~ We gave
the phone to them.

It may seem strange in English for both an indirect object and its indirect object pronoun to appear in one sentence. It is not in Spanish. This is sometimes necessary because the pronoun doesn't really indicate the gender of the object. Did you notice that there is only one indirect object pronoun for the third person both male and female?

ADJECTIVES

As you know, adjectives are words describing nouns. In English, we usually place the adjective before the noun. In Spanish however, the adjectives are usually placed after the noun.

Spanish	**English**
noun + adjective	adjective + noun
Maria hermosa	~ beautiful Maria
Jorge joven	~ young Jorge

In addition to this difference, Spanish adjectives unlike those in English follow gender and number rules. They can be either singular or plural, masculine

51

or feminine depending on the noun they are describing. Let us look further using the Spanish adjectives provided above

hermoso ~ hermosa

The question is how do you change adjectives from singular to plural, from masculine to feminine? Let us look at Spanish adjectives in groups.

1. Adjectives ending in –O

The first and most common kind of Spanish adjectives are those that end with **-o.** Adjectives that fall under this category have four forms: masculine, feminine, singular and plural. If you remember our lesson on nouns, an **–o** ending is usually masculine. You turn it into feminine by replacing **–o** with **–a.** As for the plural form, all you need to do is add **–s.**

*alt**o***   *alt**a***   *alt**os***
     *alt**as***

el chico alto   *la chica alta*   *los chicos altos*   *las chicas altas*

(the tall boy)   (the tall girl)   (the tall boys)   (the tall girls)

*roj**o***   *roj**a***   *roj**os***
     *roj**as***

el libro rojo   *la pluma roja*   *los libros rojos las plumas rojas* (the red book)   (the red pen)   (the   red books)   (the red pens)

Notice in the above examples that the adjective follow the gender and number of the nouns they describe. A masculine noun gets a masculine adjective and so forth. Let us look at other example adjectives under this category.

	Masculine		Feminine	
	Singular	Plural	Singular	Plural
short	*bajo*	*bajos*	*baja*	*bajas*
brown	*moreno*	*morenos*	*morena*	*morenas*
blond	*rubio*	*rubios*	*rubia*	*rubias*
thin	*delgado*	*delgados*	*delgada*	*delgadas*
skinny	*flaco*	*flacos*	*flaca*	*flacas*
fat	*gordo*	*gordos*	*gorda*	*gordas*
old	*viejo*	*viejos*	*vieja*	*viejas*
new	*nuevo*	*nuevos*	*nueva*	*nuevas*
handsome	*guapo*	*guapos*	*guapa*	*guapas*
ugly	*feo*	*feos*	*fea*	*feas*
good	*bueno*	*buenos*	*buena*	*buenas*
bad	*malo*	*malos*	*mala*	*malas*
boring	*aburrido*	*aburridos*	*aburrida*	*aburridas*
fun	*divertido*	*divertidos*	*divertida*	*divertidas*
rich	*rico*	*ricos*	*rica*	*ricas*
delicious	*delicioso*	*deliciosos*	*deliciosa*	*deliciosas*

stupid	tonto	tontos	tonta	tontas
open	abierto	abiertos	abierta	abiertas
closed	cerrado	cerrados	cerrada	cerradas
tired	cansado	cansados	cansada	cansadas
awake	despierto	despiertos	despierta	despiertas
hot	caluroso	calurosos	calurosa	calurosas
cold	frío	fríos	fría	frías
fresh	fresco	frescos	fresca	frescas
expensive	caro	caros	cara	caras
cheap	barato	baratos	barata	baratas
fast	rápido	rápidos	rápida	rápidas
slow	lento	lentos	lenta	lentas
crazy	loco	locos	loca	locas
tranquil	tranquilo	tranquilos	tranquila	tranquilas
sick	enfermo	enfermos	enferma	enfermas
healthy	sano	sanos	sana	sanas

savory/salty	salado	salados	salada	saladas
clean	limpio	limpios	limpia	limpias
dirty	sucio	sucios	sucia	sucias
dry	seco	secos	seca	secas
wet	mojado	mojados	mojada	mojadas
unfair	injusto	injustos	injusta	injustas
fair	justo	justos	justa	justas
empty	vacío	vacíos	vacía	vacías
full	lleno	llenos	llena	llenas

2. Adjectives ending in −E

Unlike the adjectives with −o ending, this group only has two forms: singular or plural. The −e ending is applicable for singular nouns both masculine and feminine. To change it to plural form, all you need to do is add −s. This group includes adjectives of nationality that share the same ending.

inteligent**e**
inteligent**es**

el chico /la chica inteligent /las chicas inteligentes   los   chicos (the intelligent boy/girl) (the intelligent boys/girls)

pobre
pobres

el hombre/la mujer   pobre
  los hombres/las mujeres pobres

(the poor man/woman) (the poor men/women)

Here are more examples of adjectives under this category.

	Singular Masculine/Femin ine	**Plural** Masculine/Femin ine
Simple	*Simple*	*simples*
Big	*Grande*	*grandes*
Sad	*Triste*	*tristes*
strong	*Fuerte*	*fuertes*
disgusting	*Repugnante*	*repugnantes*
sweet	*Dulce*	*dulces*
happy/ joyful	*Alegre*	*alegres*

friendly	Amable	amables
gentle	Apacible	apacibles
brilliant/glowing	Brillante	brillantes
comfortable	Comfortable	comfortable
ignorant	Ignorante	ignorantes
impossible	Imposible	imposibles
late/ tardy	Tarde	tardes
cowardly	Cobarde	cobardes
brave	Valiente	valientes
sensitive	Sensible	sensible
American	Estadounidense	estadounidenses
Costa Rican	Costarricense	costarricenses
Canadian	Canadiense	Canadienses

3. Adjectives ending in consonants

Just like the adjectives with −e ending, this group only has two forms: singular and plural. The consonant ending applies for singular nouns both masculine and feminine. To change it to plural form, you must add-**es** to the end of the word.

popular
*popular**es***

el hombre/la mujer   popular hombres/las mujeres populares

los

(the popular man/woman) men/women)

(the popular

<u>*débil*</u>
<u>*débiles*</u>

el chico/la chica débil mujeres débiles

los   hombres/las

(the weak boy/girl) weak boy/girl)

(the

Let us look at more examples.

	Singular Masculine/Feminine	**Plural** Masculine/Feminine
loyal	*Fiel*	*fieles*
cheerful	*Jovial*	*joviales*
young	*Joven*	*jovenes*
cruel	*Cruel*	*crueles*
emotional	*Emocional*	*emocionales*

special	*Especial*	*especiales*
formal	*Formal*	*formales*
fragile	*Frágil*	*fragile*
useless	*Inútil*	*inútiles*
useful	*Útil*	*útiles*
better	*Major*	*mejores*
natural	*Natural*	*Naturals*
rude	*Vulgar*	*vulgares*

*There are a few exceptions to this rule. Adjectives ending in **-or**, **-án**, **-ón**, or **–ín** have more than two forms. That's because they have a feminine form.

	Masculine		**Feminine**	
	Singular	Plural	Singular	Plural
charming	*encanta dor*	*encantad ores*	*encanta dora*	*encantad oras*
talkative	*hablado r*	*hablador es*	*hablado ra*	*Hablador as*
hardworking	*trabaja dor*	*trabajad ores*	*trabajad ora*	*Trabajad oras*

4. Adjectives of nationality

Most adjectives of nationality end in −o or −a. In this case, they follow the same rules as the first group. They have four forms. Here is an example.

mexicano   *mexicana*   *mexicanos*
     mexicanas

el hombre mexicano   ~ the Mexican man

la mujer mexicana   ~ the Mexican woman

los hombres mexicanos   ~ the Mexican men

las mujeres mexicanas ~ the Mexican women

	Masculine		Feminine	
	Singular Plural		Singular	Plural
Australian	*australiano*	*australianos*	*australiana*	*Australianas*
Chilean	*chileno*	*chilenos*	*chilena*	*Chilenas*
Puerto Rican	*puertorriqueño*	*puertorriqueños*	*puertorriqueña*	*puertorriqueñas*
Italian	*italiano*	*italianos*	*italiana*	*Italianas*
Argentinian	*argentino*	*argentinos*	*argentina*	*Argentinas*

There are a couple of adjectives of nationality that end in consonants. And they have four forms: masculine, feminine, singular and plural. The adjective ending in consonant is masculine singular. Add −es to the end to make it masculine plural. To change into singular feminine, add −a in the end and for the feminine plural form, add −as.

español   *española*   *español**es***
   *español**as***

el hombre español ~ the Spanish man

*la mujer españo**la*** ~ the Spanish woman

*los hombres españo**les*** ~ the Spanish men

*las mujeres españo**las*** ~ the Spanish women

Checkout a few more examples and pay attention to the changes in the accented vowels.

	Masculine Singular Plural		**Feminine** Singular Plural	
French	*francés*	*franceses*	*francesa*	*francesas*
German	*alemán*	*alemanos*	*alemana*	*alemanas*
Thai	*tailandés*	*tailandeses*	*tailandesa*	*tailandesas*
Lebanes	*libanés*	*libaneses*	*libanesa*	*libanesas*

e				
Japanese	*japonés*	*japoneses*	*japonesa*	*japonesas*
Irish	*irlandés*	*irlandeses*	*irlandesa*	*irlandesas*
Finnish	*finlandés*	*finlandeses*	*finlandesa*	*finlandesas*
Danish	*danés*	*daneses*	*danesa*	*Danesas*

Now compare the above examples with these below. Take note of the accented vowel.

	Masculine Singular Plural		Feminine Singular Plural	
Moroccan	*marroquí*	*marroquíes*	*marroquí*	*marroquíes*
Iraqi	*iraquí*	*iraquíes*	*iraquí*	*iraquíes*
Indian	*hindú*	*hindúes*	*hindú*	*Hindúes*

5. Adjectives of quantity

These are adjectives that indicate the quantity of a noun. In English, we have "a few," "some," "many," etc. The main difference between descriptive adjectives and adjectives of quantity is that while the former usually comes after the noun, the latter is placed before the noun.

	Masculine Singular Plural		Feminine Singular Plural	
some/any	algún	algúnos	algúna	algúnas
many/ much	mucho	muchos	mucha	muchas
few/ little	poco	pocos	poca	pocas
so many/ so much	tanto	tantos	tanta	tantas
all/ every/ each	todo	todos	toda	todas
enough/sufficient	bastante		bastantes	
Both	-	ambos	-	ambas
some	-	unos	-	unas
several	-	varios	-	varias
No	ningún	-	ninguna	-

Although most adjectives are placed after the noun, adjectives of quantity are an exception. As you will see in the examples below, they are used before the noun they describe. There are a few more exceptions to the adjective placement rule and you will get to know them in the next lessons.

Examples:

alguna vez   ~
some time

varios coches   ~
several cars

algunos años
~ some years

varias casas
~ several houses

algunas   personas
~ a few people

unos perros
~ some dogs

mucho trabajo   ~
many/ much work

unas madres
~ some mothers

mucha energía   ~
much energy

"To Be" Verbs *SER / ESTAR*

Now you know nouns, pronouns and adjectives. Let us try to formulate simple sentences using what you have learned so far. For this, you need verbs.

Both of these Spanish verbs mean "to be" however, they are conjugated differently. Another difference between the two is in their usage. Examine how they are conjugated first.

Subject	SER	ESTAR	
Yo	Soy	Estoy	I am
Tu	Eres	Estás	You are (informal)
El Ella Usted	Es	está	He is She is You are (formal)
Nosotros Nosotras	Somos	estamos	We are (masculine) We are (feminine)
Vosotros Vosotras	Sois	estáis	You all (M, informal) You all (F, informal)
Ellos Ellas Ustedes	Son	están	They are They are You all are (formal)

SER is used for objects or persons that remain unchanged. For those reason, we use **Yo soy...** when asked about our name or country of origin.

Yo soy Maria. ~ I am Maria.

Yo soy española. ~ I am Spanish.

Los chicos estadounidenses. ~ The boys are Americans.

SER is also used when talking about where and when an event may take place.

La fiesta es en mi casa. ~ The party is at my house.

La fiesta es en martes. ~ The party is on Tuesday.

While **SER** is used for more permanent things or state, **ESTAR** is used for temporary ones. For instance, when someone asks how you are doing, you use **ESTAR** simply because you are speaking about the present and what you feeling at the moment may change in the future.

(Yo) estoy bien. ~ I am fine.

Jorge está hambriento. ~ Jorge is hungry.

Las chicas están alegres. ~ The girls are happy.

Chapter 5 – Asking Questions

It is not just about knowing how to answer questions, knowing how to ask questions is just as equally important or understanding them at the very least. In this chapter, you will get to know basic question words to help you clarify matters and or point things out. Before that, let us get to know the Spanish word *hay*.

USES of *HAY*

This word comes from **haber**, meaning "to have." We use it to say "there is" or "there are." This means *hay* is in the present tense and may be used to refer to one or more things. **Habia** is the past tense form, meaning "there was" or "there were" but we will save that for later.

Hay un gato fuera. ~ There is a cat outside.
outside.

Hay unos gatos fuera. ~ There are cats outside.

Based on these examples, you can conclude that *hay* is used for making general or passive observations. While it is correct to say, "There are books on the table," it is not proper to use hay to say, "there they are (the books)" or "there are the books, right there on the table." Otherwise, you are already referring to something specific and *hay* is only reserved for unspecific things. It is also good to point out that **hay** is only used for indefinite articles, never for definite articles. However, hay does not necessarily require them.

We can also use hay for asking questions. When you intend to ask a question, hay could mean "is there" or "are there."

¿Hay un gato fuera?	~ Is there a cat outside?
¿Hay gatos fuera?	~ Are there cats outside?
¿Hay un perro ladrando?	~ Is there a dog barking?
¿Hay perros ladrando?	~ Are there dogs barking?

THE INTERROGATIVES

There are 8 basic interrogative question words and they are the following:

¿quién?	~ Who?
¿qué?	~ What?
¿cuándo?	~ When?
¿dónde?	~ Where?
¿por qué?	~ Why?

¿cómo?	~ How?
¿cuánto?	~ How much/ how many?
¿cuál?	~ Which?

There are specific rules for using each of them. For now, let us stick with rules that apply to them in general. One, please remember that when using these question words, the subject must go after the verb. As for pronunciation, the accents in these interrogatives do not affect the way the words are pronounced. Rather, they indicate the syllable that needs to be emphasized.

You may have also noticed the inverted question mark before the word. This is important in written Spanish just as an inverted exclamation point is required for writing sentences.

¿Quién? (WHO)

Obviously, this is the interrogative to use to find out someone's identity. ¿Quién? is used to refer to singular subjects. Add -es in the end and you have its plural form, ¿Quiénes?, which always goes with the verb SER. Please refer to the examples below and the conjugation for the irregular verb SER for your reference.

Irregular Verb SER Conjugation

Subject	SER	

Yo	*Soy*	I am
Tu	*Eres*	You are (informal)
El *Ella* *Usted*	*Es*	He is She is You are (formal)
Nosotros *Nosotras*	*Somos*	We are (masculine) We are (feminine)
Vosotros *Vosotras*	*Sois*	You all (M, informal) You all (F, informal)
Ellos *Ellas* *Ustedes*	*Son*	They are They are You all are (formal)

¿Quién es?   ~ Who is it?

¿Quiénes son esas personas?   ~ Who are these people?

There are variations to this interrogative. Pay attention to the following.

¿A quién? or ¿A quiénes? ("to whom" or "for whom")

Use **¿A quién?** when the indirect object is singular and **¿A quiénes?** if it is plural.

¿A quién pertenece a esta bolsa?

> ~ To whom does this bag belong to?/ Who does this bag belong to?

¿A quiénes son estas flores para?

> ~ For whom are these flowers?/ Who are these flowers for?

¿Con quién? or ¿Con quiénes? ("with whom")

Use this variation when there are two or more people implied in the conversation.

¿Con quién te vas?

> ~ With whom are you leaving?/ Who are you leaving with?

¿Con quiénes bailando Jorge?

> ~ With whom is Jorge dancing?/ Who is Jorge dancing with?

¿De quién? or ¿De quiénes? ("whose")

¿De quién es esta bolsa?   ~ Whose bag is this?

¿De quiénes son estos libros?   ~   Whose books are these?

¿Qué? (WHAT)

Use this interrogative if you want to seek an explanation or definition. It remains unchanged whether it is used to refer to a singular or plural subject. There is only one variation, **¿De qué?** which means "of what" or "about what."

¿Qué libro es su favorito? ~ What book is your favorite?

¿Qué vas a hacer mañana? ~ What are you doing tomorrow?

¿De qué es el libro? ~ What is the book about?

¿De qué material está hecha la bolsa? ~ What material is the bad made of?

¿Cuándo? (WHEN)

This form is applicable for both singular and plural subjects.

¿Cuándo es tu cumpleaños? ~ When is your birthday?

¿Cuándo estás tomando un viaje? ~ When are you taking a trip?

¿Dónde? (WHERE)

This interrogative is used for determining the location of an object. It applies for both singular and plural objects. **¿De dónde?** ("from where") is used for identifying a noun's origin. **¿Adónde?** on the other hand, means "to where" for identifying a destination. **¿Adónde?** always goes with the verb **IR**, meaning "to go." Examples are provided below along with reference to the conjugation of the irregular verb **IR**.

Irregular Verb IR Conjugation

Subject	IR	
Yo	Voy	I go
Tu	Vas	You go (informal)
El Ella Usted	Va	He goes She goes You go (formal)
Nosotros Nosotras	Vamos	We go (masculine) We go (feminine)
Vosotros Vosotras	Váis	You all go (M, informal) You all go (F, informal)
Ellos Ellas Ustedes	Van	They go They go You all go (formal)

¿Donde está el gato?   ~ Where is the cat?

¿Dónde están los perros? ~ Where are the dogs?

¿De dónde está María? ~ Where is Maria from?

¿De dónde eres? ~ Where are you from?

¿Adónde va este autobús? ~ Where does this bus go to?

¿Adónde están los chicos que van a este fin de semana?

~ Where are the boys going to this weekend?

¿Por qué? (WHY/FOR WHAT REASON)

Do not confuse this interrogative with **porque** which means "because." While **¿Por qué?** is meant to identify a reason, **¿Para qué?** is the interrogative to use if you want to find out a purpose. **¿Para qué?** means "for what purpose."

¿Por qué el estudio de Maria? ~ For what reason/ why does Maria study?

Porque María quiere aprender. ~ Because Maria wants to learn.

¿Para qué el estudio de Maria? ~ For what purpose/ why does Maria study?

Para obtener una alta puntuación en el examen

~ In order to get a high score in the exam

¿Cómo? (HOW)

This interrogative can be used for both singular and plural subjects. *¿Cómo?* can also be used to clarify something. In this case, it can mean "Can you say it again?" or "Can you repeat that?"

¿Cómo está usted? ~ How are you?

¿Cómo es esto posible? ~ How is this possible?

¿Cómo se explica que en español? ~ How do you explain it in Spanish?

¿Cuánto? (HOW MUCH/ HOW MANY)

There are four forms for this interrogative. And they are the following.

¿Cuánto? For masculine singular nouns

¿Cuánto? For masculine plural nouns

¿Cuánta? For feminine singular nouns

¿Cuántas? For feminine plural nouns

¿Cuánto cuesta esta camisa? ~ How much for this shirt?

¿Cuántos por estas camisas? ~ How much for these shirts?

¿Cuántas casas tienen? ~ How many houses do they have?

¿Cuántos coches tiene que conducir? ~ How many cars does he drive?

¿Cuál? (WHICH)

This interrogative is used to ask for a choice given different possibilities or from a selection. *¿Cuál?* is the singular form. *¿Cuáles?* is the plural form. When this interrogative is combined with the verb SER in a sentence, it can also mean "what?"

¿Cuál de sus canciones te gusta más? ~ Which of their songs do you like best?

¿Cuálas los libros me recomiendan? ~ Which books do you recommend?

That concludes this chapter but before we proceed with the next lesson, let us have a quick review of the lessons we have covered.

	Masculine Singular Plural	Feminine Singular Plural
There is/ are	*Hay*	
There was/ were	*Habia*	
Is/ Are there?	*¿Hay?*	
Who?	*¿Quién? + SER*	*¿Quiénes? + SER*
To/ For whom?	*¿A quién?*	*¿A quiénes?*
With whom?	*¿Con quién?*	*¿Con quiénes?*
Whose?	*¿De quién?*	*¿De quiénes?*
What?	*¿Qué?*	
Of/	*¿De qué?*	

About what?	
When?	*¿Cuándo?*
Where?	*¿Dónde?*
From where?	*¿De dónde?*
Where to?	*¿Adónde? + IR*
For what reason/ why?	*¿Por qué?*
Because	*Porque*
For what purpose?	*¿Para qué?*
How?	*¿Cómo?*

How much?/ How many?	¿Cuánto?	¿Cuántos?	¿Cuánta?	¿Cuántas?
Which?	¿Cuál?		¿Cuáles?	

Chapter 6 – Regular and Irregular Verbs

Just like in English, the Spanish language has both regular and irregular verbs. To put simply, regular verbs follow a specific pattern for conjugation. That means they are predictable. As long as you understand the pattern, you can conjugate any regular verbs. Irregular verbs on the other hand, do not follow any rules. And since you cannot predict their conjugation based on a pattern, you need to memorize them instead.

In general, Spanish verbs, both regular and irregular, can be grouped according to their suffix. These are −AR, -ER and −IR.

REGULAR VERBS

Let's focus on regular verbs first.

To conjugate regular Spanish verbs ending in −AR, -ER and −IR, you need to drop these ending and attach a suffix according to which agrees with the subject.

How to Conjugate Regular −AR Verbs

You can refer to the table below indicating what suffixes to use for which subject.

Subject	-AR

Yo	**-o**
Tu	**-as**
El Ella Usted (Formal you)	**-a**
Nosotros Nosotras	**-amos**
Vosotros Vosotras (Informal you all)	**-aís**
Ellos Ellas Ustedes (Formal you all)	**-an**

A few examples of Spanish verbs ending in **−AR** are **CANTAR** (to sing) and **BAILAR** (to dance). Now, observe how they are conjugated.

Subject	*CANTAR*	*BAILAR*	
Yo	canto	bailo	I sing/ dance
Tu	cantas	bailas	You sing/ dance
El Ella Usted (Formal you)	canta	baila	He sings/ dances She sings/ dances It sings/ dances
Nosotros Nosotras	cantamos	bailamos	We sing/ dance

Vosotros *Vosotras* (Informal you all)	*cant***aís**	*bail***aís**	You all sing/ dance
Ellos *Ellas* *Ustedes* (Formal you all)	*cant***an**	*bail***an**	They sing/ dance

Here are a few more Spanish verbs ending in **-AR**. You can try to conjugate them in the present tense based on your observations from above.

arreglar ~ to repair

aceptar ~ to accept

caminar ~ to walk

llevar ~ to carry

terminar ~ to finish

esperar ~ to wait

parar ~ to stop

buscar ~ to look for

llegar ~ to arrive

escuchar ~ to listen

llamar ~ to call

(Yo) arreglo el radio roto. ~ I repair the broken television.

(Tu) aceptas la invitación. ~ You accept the invitation.

Jorge camina con Maria.   ~ Jorge walks with Maria.

Maria lleva el equipaje pesado.   ~ Maria carries the heavy luggage.

La película empeza a las 3:00 de la tarde.

~ The movie begins at 3:00 in the afternoon.

(Nosotros) terminamos el trabajo temprano hoy.

~ We finish work early today.

(Vosotras) esperáis al maestro.   ~ You (girls) wait for the teacher.

(Vosotros) paráis de burlarse de ella.   ~ You (boys) stop teasing her.

La clase busca pistas.   ~ The class looks for clues.

Los soldados llegan hoy.   ~ The soldiers arrive today.

Los niños escuchan bien.   ~ The children listen well.

Por favor llama a este número señor.   ~ Please call this number, sir.

How to Conjugate Regular –ER Verbs

You can refer to the table below indicating what suffixes to use for which subject.

Subject	-ER
Yo	-o
Tu	-es
El Ella Usted (Formal you)	-e
Nosotros Nosotras	-emos
Vosotros Vosotras (Informal you all)	-eís
Ellos Ellas Ustedes (Formal you all)	-en

A few examples of Spanish verbs ending in −**AR** are **BEBER** (to drink) and **COMER** (to eat). And this is how they are conjugated.

Subject	BEBER	COMER	
Yo	bebo	como	I drink/ eat
Tu	bebes	comes	You drink/ eat
El Ella Usted (Formal	bebe	come	He drinks/ eats She drinks/ eats

you)			It drinks/ eats
Nosotros *Nosotras*	*beb***emos**	*com***emos**	We drink/ eat
Vosotros *Vosotras* (Informal you all)	*beb***eís**	*com***eís**	You all drink/ eat
Ellos *Ellas* *Ustedes* (Formal you all)	*beb***en**	*com***eís**	They drink/ eat

Here are a few more Spanish verbs ending in **−ER** and a few sentence examples using them.

leer	~ to read	*prometer* ~ to promise	
aprender	~ to learn		
vender	~ to sell	*perder*	~ to lose
correr run	~ to	*romper*	~ to break
		creer	~ to believe

(Yo) bebo un vaso de leche cada noche. ~ I drink a glass of milk every night.

(Tu) comes toda la comida sobrante. ~ You eat all the leftover food.

Juan lee la Biblia todos los días. ~ Juan reads
the Bible every day.

Petra aprende mucho de la clase. ~ Petra
learns a lot from class.

(Nosotros) vendemos recuerdos hechos a mano.

~ We sell
handcrafted souvenirs.

Las mujeres y me corremos el maratón juntos.

~ The women and I run
the marathon together.

(Vosotros) prometeís a comportarse. ~ You (boys)
promise to behave.

(Vosotras) perdeís cada año. ~ You (girls)
lose every year.

(Ellos) rompen las leyes todo el tiempo. ~ They
break laws all the time.

(Ustedes) creen en la biblia. ~ (You all) believe
in the Bible.

How to Conjugate Regular –IR Verbs

You can refer to the table below indicating what
suffixes to use for which subject. You may notice that
the pattern of conjugation for **–ER** and **–IR** verbs
are almost the same except for the subject
Nosotros/ Nosotras.

Subject	-IR
Yo	-o
Tu	-es
El Ella Usted (Formal you)	-e
Nosotros Nosotras	-imos
Vosotros Vosotras (Informal you all)	-eís
Ellos Ellas Ustedes (Formal you all)	-en

A few examples of Spanish verbs ending in **–IR** are **ESCRIBIR** (to write) and **ABRIR** (to open). Now, observe how they are conjugated.

Subject	*ESCRIBIR*	*ABRIR*	
Yo	escri**bo**	ab**ro**	I write/ open
Tu	escrib**es**	ab**res**	You write/ open
El Ella Usted (Formal you)	escrib**e**	ab**re**	He writes/ opens She writes/ opens It writes/ opens

Nosotros Nosotras	escrib**imos**	ab**imos**	We write/ open
Vosotros Vosotras (Informal you all)	escrib**éis**	abr**éis**	You all write/ open
Ellos Ellas Ustedes (Formal you all)	escrib**en**	abr**en**	They write/ open

You will find more Spanish verbs ending in −**IR** and a few sentence examples below.

describir ~ to describe

asistir ~ to attend

permitir ~ to allow

conducir ~ to drive

recibir ~ to receive

oír ~ to hear

decidir ~ to decide

vivir ~ to live

(Yo) escribo cartas para él. ~ I write letters for him.

(Tu) abres la puerta para mí. ~ (You) open the door for me.

(Ella) describe la pintura tan bien. ~ She describes the painting so well.

(Nosotros) atendimos a los huéspedes. ~ We attend to the guests.

(Ellos) permiten mascotas dentro del hotel. ~ They allow pets inside the hotel.

El señor Domínguez conduce un coche de lujo.

~ Mister Dominguez drives a fancy car.

(Ellos) reciben pedidos por teléfono. ~ They receive orders over the phone.

(Nosotros) oímos rumores sobre ti. ~ We hear rumors about you.

El tribunal decide sobre el caso hoy en día.

~ The court decides on the case today.

Vive usted vida al máximo. ~ Live your life to the fullest.

IRREGULAR VERBS

We've covered present tense conjugation of a few irregular verbs from lessons in the previous chapters. So far, you are familiar with these verbs.

ESTAR ~ To Be

SER ~ To Be

IR ~ To Go

We will now look at more examples. Remember that you have to memorize these conjugations since irregular verbs do not follow any patterns.

Haber and *Tener* ("to have")

Both verbs mean "to have" but each has specific uses. There are more differences than similarities between the two. For now, let's stick with the basics. *Tener* is used to indicate possession. *Haber* is more often used as an auxiliary verb which simply means it needs to be partnered with another verb. Otherwise, it does not carry any meaning.

	TENER	*HABER*	
Yo	*tengo*	*he*	I have
Tu	*tienes*	*has*	You have
El *Ella* *Usted* (Formal you)	*tiene*	*ha* *hay*	He/she/it has
Nosotros *Nosotras*	*tenemos*	*hemos*	We have
Vosotros *Vosotras*	*tenías*	*habeís*	You (all) have

(Informal you all)			
Ellos Ellas Ustedes (Formal you all)	**tienen**	**han**	They have

Here are a few examples focusing on what is most useful for now, **Tener**.

(Yo) tengo un bolígrafo.　　　　~ I have a pen.

(Tu) tienes una manzana.　　　~ You have an apple.

(Nosotros) tenemos la piña. ~ We have pineapple.

Hacer ("to make" or "to do")

	HACER	
Yo	**hago**	I make/ do
Tu	**haces**	You make/ do
El Ella Usted (Formal you)	**hace**	He/she/it makes/ does
Nosotros Nosotras	**hacemos**	We make/ do
Vosotros Vosotras	**hacéis**	You (all) make/ do

(Informal you all)		
Ellos *Ellas* *Ustedes* (Formal you all)	**hacen**	They make/ do

María hace galletas. ~ Maria makes cookies.

Los estudiantes hacen la tarea. ~ The students do homework.

Por favor, (usted) hace trabajo. ~ Please do your job.

Poder ("to be able to" or "can")

Ver ("to see")

Decir ("to say" or "to tell")

	PODER	**VER**	**DECIR**
Yo	**puedo**	**veo**	**digo**
Tu	**puedes**	**ves**	**dices**
El *Ella* *Usted* (Formal you)	**puede**	**ve**	**dice**
Nosotros *Nosotras*	**podemos**	**vemos**	**decimos**

Vosotros Vosotras (Informal you all)	**podeís**	**veís**	**decís**
Ellos Ellas Ustedes (Formal you all)	**pueden**	**ven**	**dicen**

(Nosotros) podemos ganar el juego. ~ We are able to win the game.

(Yo) veo un avión. ~ I see a plane.

(Ellos) dicen mentiras. ~ They tell lies.

Querer ("to want" or "to love")

Dar ("to give")

Saber ("to know" information)

Conocer ("to know" people and places)

	QUERER	**DAR**	**SABER**	**CONOCER**
Yo	**Quiero**	**doy**	**sé**	**conozco**
Tu	**Quieres**	**das**	**sabes**	**conoces**
El Ella	**Quiere**	**da**	**sabe**	**conoce**

Usted (Formal you)				
Nosotros Nosotras	Queremos	damos	sabemos	conocemos
Vosotros Vosotras (Informal you all)	Quereís	dais	sabeís	conoceís
Ellos Ellas Ustedes (Formal you all)	Quiren	dan	saben	conocen

(Yo) quiero un poco de helado. ~ I want some ice cream.

(Usted) da amor el día de Navidad. ~ Give love on Christmas day.

(Nosotros) sabemos los hechos. ~ We know the facts.

(Ellos) conocen que la gente famosa. ~ They know famous people.

Venir ("to come")

Salir ("to leave" or "to go out")

Volver ("to return" or "to go back")

Poner ("to put/ place/ set")

	VENIR	*SALIR*	*VOLVER*	*PONER*
Yo	*Vengo*	*salgo*	*vuelvo*	*pongo*
Tu	*Vienes*	*sales*	*vuelves*	*pones*
El Ella Usted (Formal you)	*Viene*	*sale*	*vuelve*	*pone*
Nosotros Nosotras	*Venimos*	*salimos*	*volvemos*	*ponemos*
Vosotros Vosotras (Informal you all)	*Venís*	*salís*	*volveis*	*poneis*
Ellos Ellas Ustedes (Formal	*Vienen*	*salen*	*volven*	*ponen*

you all)				

Aqui (ellos) vienen. come.   ~ Here they

Mi hermana y mi salimos hoy. and I leave today.   ~ My sister

(Yo) vuelvo a conocerlo. meet you.   ~ I return to

(Ustedes) ponen las bolsas en el frente para la inspección.

~ Place your bags in front for inspection.

Seguir ("to follow" or "to continue")

Parecer ("to appear" or "to seem")

Contar ("to count" or "to relate")

Encontrar ("to find" or "to encounter")

	SEGUIR	*PARECER*	*CONTAR*	*ENCONTRAR*
Yo	*sigo*	*parezco*	*cuento*	*encuentro*
Tu	*sigues*	*pareces*	*cuentas*	*encuentras*
El	*sigue*	*parece*	*cuenta*	*encuentra*

Ella Usted (Formal you)				
Nosotros Nosotras	**seguimos**	**parecemos**	**contamos**	**encontramos**
Vosotros Vosotras (Informal you all)	**seguís**	**parecéis**	**contaís**	**encontreís**
Ellos Ellas Ustedes (Formal you all)	**siguen**	**parecen**	**cuentan**	**encuentran**

(Usted) sigue el mapa.   ~ You follow the map.

Jorge parece estar perdido.   ~ He seems to be lost.

(Ellos) cuentan los turistas.   ~ They count the tourists.

Lo (yo) encuentro interesante.   ~ I find him interesting.

Sentir ("to feel" or "to regret")

Recordar ("to remember" or "to remind")

Empezar ("to begin/start")

Entender ("to understand")

	SENTIR	RECORDAR	EMPEZAR	ENTENDER
Yo	siento	recuerdo	empiezo	entiendo
Tu	sienties	recuerdas	empiezas	entiendes
El Ella Usted (Formal you)	sentie	recuerda	empieza	Entiende
Nosotros Nosotras	sentimos	recodamos	empezamos	entendemos
Vosotros Vosotras (Informal you all)	sentís	recordáis	empezaís	entendeís
Ellos	siente	recuerda	empieza	entiende

Ellas Ustedes (Formal you all)	n	n	n	n

(Yo) siento triste. ~ I feel sleepy.

(Nosotros) recordamos todo lo. ~ We remember everything.

(Él) empieza a preguntarse. ~ He begins to wonder.

Los niños entienden. ~ The children understand.

Chapter 7 – Let's Look at the Past

Congratulations! You're getting the hang of it.

You are now familiar about creating sentences in the present. But what if you want to talk about the past? The Spanish past tense has many different foms. But since you are a beginner, we will focus on Preterite so you can talk about events that are already completed. And yes, you will need to conjugate the verbs, particularly in the Preterite. To facilitate better learning, we will use the same examples as provided in the previous chapter.

Let us begin!

How to Conjugate Regular –AR Verbs

As you look at the new word endings below, you will find a few differences and some similarities between the Preterite and the Present tense. As long as you know these endings by heart, you can convert any regular Spanish verb with an **–AR** ending.

Subject	-AR
Yo	**-é**
Tu	**-aste**
El *Ella* *Usted* (Formal you)	**-ó**

Nosotros Nosotras	-amos
Vosotros Vosotras (Informal you all)	-asteis
Ellos Ellas Ustedes (Formal you all)	-aron

Look at the table below to understand how **CANTAR** (to sing) and **BAILAR** (to dance) are conjugated.

Subject	*CANTAR*	*BAILAR*	
Yo	cant**é**	bail**é**	I sang/ danced
Tu	cant**aste**	bail**aste**	You sang/ danced
El Ella Usted (Formal you)	cant**o**	bail**o**	He sang/ danced She sang/ danced It sang/ danced
Nosotros Nosotras	cant**amos**	bail**amos**	We sang/ danced
Vosotros Vosotras (Informal you all)	cant**astais**	bail**astais**	You all sang/ danced
Ellos Ellas Ustedes	cant**aron**	bail**aron**	They sang/ danced

(Formal you all)			

Look at the other **−AR** ending verbs again and how they are used in the past tense.

arreglar ~ to repair

aceptar ~ to accept

caminar ~ to walk

llevar ~ to carry

terminar ~ to finish

esperar ~ to wait

parar ~ to stop

buscar ~ to look for

llegar ~ to arrive

escuchar ~ to listen

llamar ~ to call

(Yo) arreglé el radio roto. ~ I repaired the broken television.

(Tu) aceptaste la invitación. ~ You accepted the invitation.

Jorge camino con Maria. ~ Jorge walked with Maria.

Maria llevo el equipaje pesado. ~ Maria carried the heavy luggage.

(Nosotros) terminamos el trabajo temprano hoy.

~ We finished work early today.

(Vosotras) esperastais al maestro. ~ You (girls) waited for the teacher.

(Vosotros) parastais de burlarse de ella. ~ You (boys) stopped teasing her.

La clase busco pistas. ~ The class looked for clues.

Los soldados llegaron hoy. ~ The soldiers arrived today.

Los niños escucharon bien. ~ The children listened well.

Por favor llamo a este número señor. ~ Please call this number, sir.

How to Conjugate Regular –ER and –IR Verbs

Now, here's something different. The Preterite conjugation of regular verbs ending in **–ER** and **–IR** are the same.

Subject	-ER/ -IR
Yo	**-í**
Tu	**-iste**
El *Ella* *Usted* (Formal you)	**-ió**

Nosotros Nosotras	**-imos**
Vosotros Vosotras (Informal you all)	**-isteis**
Ellos Ellas Ustedes (Formal you all)	**-ieron**

BEBER (to drink) and *COMER* (to eat)

Subject	*BEBER*	*COMER*	
Yo	*bebí*	*comí*	I drank/ ate
Tu	*bebiste*	*comiste*	You drank/ ate
El *Ella* *Usted* *(Formal you)*	*bebió*	*Comió*	He drank/ ate She drank/ ate It drank/ ate
Nosotros *Nosotras*	*bebimos*	*Comimos*	We drank/ ate
Vosotros *Vosotras* *(Informal you all)*	*bebisteis*	*Comisteis*	You all drank/ ate
Ellos *Ellas* *Ustedes* *(Formal you all)*	*bebieron*	*Comieron*	They drank/ ate

Other -ER Verbs in Preterite

leer	~ to read	*prometer*	~ to promise
aprender	~ to learn	*perder*	~ to lose
vender	~ to sell	*romper*	~ to break
correr	~ to run	*creer*	~ to believe

(Yo) bebí un vaso de leche. ~ I drank a glass of milk.

(Tu) comiste toda la comida sobrante. ~ You ate all the leftover food.

Juan leyó la Biblia. ~ Juan read the Bible.

Petra aprendió mucho de la clase. ~ Petra learned a lot from class.

(Nosotros) vendímos recuerdos hechos a mano. ~ We sold handcrafted souvenirs.

Las mujeres y me corrímos el maratón juntos. ~ The women and I ran the marathon together.

(Vosotros) prometisteis a comportarse. ~ You (boys) promised to behave.

(Vosotras) perdisteis de nuevo.   ~ You (girls)
lost again.

(Ellos) romperon la ley.   ~   They
broke the law.

(Ustedes) creeron en la biblia.   ~ (You all)
believed in the Bible.

Abrir ("to open") and *Escribir* ("to write")

Subject	ESCRIBIR	ABRIR	
Yo	*escrib**í***	*Abr**í***	I wrote/ opened
Tu	*escrib**iste***	*Abr**iste***	You wrote/ opened
El *Ella* *Usted* (Formal you)	*escrib**ió***	*abr**ió***	He wrote/ opened She wrote/ opened It wrote/ opened
Nosotros *Nosotras*	*escrib**imos***	*Abr**imos***	We wrote/ opened
Vosotros *Vosotras* (Informal you all)	*escrib**isteis***	*abr**isteis***	You all wrote/ opened
Ellos *Ellas* *Ustedes* (Formal	*escrib**eron***	*abr**eron***	They wrote/ opened

you all)			

Other –IR ending verbs in Preterite

describir ~ to describe   *recibir* ~ to receive

asistir ~ to attend   *oír* ~ to hear

permitir ~ to allow   *decidir* ~ to decide

conducir ~ to drive   *vivir* ~ to live

(Yo) escribí cartas para él. ~ I wrote letters for him.

(Tu) abriste la puerta para mí. ~ (You) opened the door for me.

(Ella) describió la pintura tan bien. ~ She described the painting so well.

(Nosotros) atendímos a los huéspedes. ~ We attended to the guests.

(Ellos) permiteron mascotas dentro del hotel.

~ They allowed pets inside the hotel.

El señor Domínguez condució un coche de lujo.

~ Mister Dominguez drove a fancy car.

(Ellos) reciberon pedidos por teléfono. ~ They received orders over the phone.

(Nosotros) oímos rumores sobre ti. ~ We heard rumors about you.

El tribunal decidió sobre el caso hoy en día.

~ The court decided on the case today.

(El) vivió su vida al máximo. ~ He lived his life to the fullest.

IRREGULAR VERBS

We've already covered the present tense conjugation of ESTAR, SER and IR. Now, let's see how they look in their Preterite conjugation.

ESTAR ("to be")

SER ("to be")

IR ("to go")

	ESTAR	*SER*	*IR*
Yo	*estuve*	*Fui*	*fui*
Tu	*estuviste*	*Fuiste*	*fuiste*
El *Ella* *Usted* (Formal you)	*estuvo*	*Fue*	*fue*
Nosotros *Nosotras*	*estuvimos*	*Fuimos*	*fuimos*
Vosotros *Vosotras* (Informal you all)	*estuvimos*	*Fuisteis*	*fuisteis*
Ellos *Ellas* *Ustedes* (Formal you all)	*estuvieron*	*Fueron*	*fueron*

Los chicos fueron estadounidenses.   ~ The boys were Americans.

La fiesta fue en mi casa. ~ The party was at my house.

(Yo) estuve bien. ~ I was fine.

Jorge estuvo hambriento. ~ Jorge was hungry.

Las chicas estuvieron alegres. ~ The girls were happy.

(Nosotros) fuimos a su casa. ~ We went to your house.

We will now look at more examples. Remember that you have to memorize these conjugations since irregular verbs do not follow any patterns.

Tener ("to have")

Hacer ("to make" or "to do")

	TENER	HACER
Yo	tuve	hice
Tu	tuviste	Hiciste
El Ella Usted (Formal you)	tuvo	Hizo
Nosotros Nosotras	tuvimos	Hicimos

Vosotros Vosotras (Informal you all)	*tuvisteis*	*Hicisteis*
Ellos Ellas Ustedes (Formal you all)	*tuvieron*	*Hicieron*

(Yo) tuve un bolígrafo.   ~ I had a pen.

(Tu) tuviste una manzana.   ~ You had an apple.

(Nosotros) tuvimos la piña. ~ We had pineapple.

María hizo galletas.   ~ Maria made cookies.

Los estudiantes hicieron la tarea. ~ The students did homework.

Poder ("to be able to" or "can")

Ver ("to see")

Decir ("to say" or "to tell")

	PODER	VER	DECIR
Yo	*pude*	*Vi*	*dije*
Tu	*pudiste*	*Viste*	*dijiste*
El Ella Usted	*pudo*	*Vio*	*dijo*

(Formal you)			
Nosotros Nosotras	**pudimos**	**Vimos**	**dijimos**
Vosotros Vosotras (Informal you all)	**pudisteis**	**Visteis**	**dijisteis**
Ellos Ellas Ustedes (Formal you all)	**pudieron**	**Vieron**	**dijeron**

(Nosotros) pudimos ganar el juego. ~ We were able to win the game.

(Yo) vi un avión. ~ I saw a plane.

(Ellos) dijeron mentiras. ~ They told lies.

Querer ("to want" or "to love")

Dar ("to give")

Saber ("to know" information)

Conocer ("to know" people and places)

	QUERER	DAR	SABER	CONOCER
Yo	quise	Di	supe	conocí
Tu	quisiste	Diste	supiste	conociste
El Ella Usted (Formal you)	quiso	Dio	supo	conoció
Nosotros Nosotras	quisimos	dimos	supimos	conocimos
Vosotros Vosotras (Informal you all)	quisisteis	disteis	supisteis	conocisteis
Ellos Ellas Ustedes (Formal you all)	quisieron	dieron	supieron	conocieron

(Yo) quise un poco de helado.   ~ I wanted some ice cream.

(El) dio amor el día de Navidad.   ~ He gave love on Christmas day.

(Nosotros) supimos los hechos. ~ We knew the facts.

(Ellos) conocieron que la gente famosa. ~ They knew famous people.

Venir ("to come")

Salir ("to leave" or "to go out")

Volver ("to return" or "to go back")

Poner ("to put/ place/ set")

	VENIR	*SALIR*	*VOLVER*	*PONER*
Yo	*vine*	*Salí*	*volví*	*puse*
Tu	*viniste*	*saliste*	*volviste*	*pusiste*
El Ella Usted (Formal you)	*vino*	*Salió*	*volvió*	*puso*
Nosotros Nosotras	*vinimos*	*salimos*	*volvimos*	*pusimos*
Vosotros Vosotra	*vinistei*	*salistei*	*volvistei*	*pusisteis*

	s	*s*	*s*	
s (Informal you all)				
Ellos Ellas Ustedes (Formal you all)	**viniero n**	**saliero n**	**volviero n**	**pusiero n**

(Ellos) vinieron aqui. ~ They came here.

Mi hermana y mi salimos temprano. ~ My sister and I left early.

(Yo) volví a conocerlo. ~ I returned to meet you.

Los señores colocaron sus bolsas en el frente para la inspección.

  ~ The gentlemen placed their bags in front for inspection.

Seguir ("to follow" or "to continue")

Parecer ("to appear" or "to seem")

Contar ("to count" or "to relate")

Encontrar ("to find" or "to encounter")

	SEGUIR	*PARECER*	*CONTAR*	*ENCONTRAR*

Yo	seguí	parecí	conté	encontré
Tu	seguiste	pareciste	contaste	encontraste
El Ella Usted (Formal you)	siguió	pareció	contó	encontró
Nosotros Nosotras	seguimos	parecimos	contamos	encontramos
Vosotros Vosotras (Informal you all)	seguisteis	parecisteis	contasteis	encontrasteis
Ellos Ellas Ustedes (Formal you all)	siguieron	parecieron	contaron	encontraron

(Vosotros) siguisteis el mapa.   ~   You followed the map.

Jorge pareciste perdido. ~ He seemed lost.

(Ellos) contó los turistas. ~ They counted the tourists.

Lo (yo) encontré interesante. ~ I found him interesting.

Sentir ("to feel" or "to regret")

Recordar ("to remember" or "to remind")

Empezar ("to begin/start")

Entender ("to understand")

	SENTIR	*RECORDAR*	*EMPEZAR*	*ENTENDER*
Yo	**sentí**	**recordé**	**empecé**	**entendí**
Tu	**sentiste**	**recordaste**	**empezaste**	**entendiste**
El Ella Usted (Formal you)	**sintió**	**recordó**	**empezó**	**entendió**
Nosotros Nosotras	**sentimos**	**recordamos**	**empezamos**	**entendimos**
Vosotr	**sentist**	**recordas**	**empezas**	**entendis**

	eis	teis	teis	teis
os Vosotr as (Infor mal you all)				
Ellos Ellas Ustede s (Form al you all)	sintier on	recordar on	empezar on	entendie ron

(Yo) sentí triste.   ~ I felt sleepy.

(Nosotros) recordamos todo lo.   ~ We remembered everything.

(Él) empezó a preguntarse. ~ He began to wonder.

Los niños entendieron.   ~   The   children understood.

Chapter 8 - Let's Talk About the Future

We've completed our lessons on the present and past. Are you ready to take on the future? Don't worry, this will be a much easier lesson. All we need to do is take some things from the previous lessons and use them to create statements about the future.

Here's a fun fact. Did you know that you can use a verb in the present tense to talk about an event that is only about to happen? In Spanish, there are various ways to express a future event. We will discuss the simplest one in this chapter.

The Future with IR

The present tense conjugation of the verb IR can be used to create sentences that refer to future events. And this is the formula.

Conjugated **IR** + *a* + Infinitive verb

And to refresh your memory, let's bring back the IR table.

Subject	IR	
Yo	**voy**	I go/ am going to
Tu	**vas**	You go/ are going to
El Ella Usted	**va**	He goes/ is going to She goes/ is going to You go/ are going to

		(formal)
Nosotros Nosotras	vamos	We go/ are going to (masculine) We go/ are going to (feminine)
Vosotros Vosotras	váis	You all go/ are going to (M, informal) You all go/ are going to (F, informal)
Ellos Ellas Ustedes	van	They go/ are going to They go/ are going to You all go/ are going to (formal)

The infinitive is the unchanged verb with –ar, -er or –ir ending. So really, all you need here is to keep remembering how IR is conjugated. There is no need for other conjugations. Let's try a couple of examples.

(Yo) voy a arreglar el radio roto.   ~ I am going to repair the broken television.

(Tu) vas a aceptar la invitación.   ~ You are going to accept the invitation.

Jorge va a caminar con Maria.   ~ Jorge is going to walk with Maria.

La clase va a buscar pistas.   ~ The class is going to look for clues.

121

Los soldados van a llegar hoy. ~ The soldiers are going to arrive today.

Los niños van a escuchar bien. ~ The children are going to listen well.

Maria va a llevar el equipaje pesado.

~ Maria is going to carry the heavy luggage.

(Nosotros) vamos a terminar el trabajo temprano hoy.

~ We are going to finish work early today.

(Vosotras) vaís a esperar al maestro.

~ You (girls) are going to wait for the teacher.

(Vosotros) vaís a parar de burlarse de ella.

~ You (boys) are going to stop teasing her.

(Yo) voy a beber un vaso de leche cada noche.

~ I am going to drink a glass of milk every night.

(Tu) vas a comer toda la comida sobrante.

~ You are going to eat all the leftover food.

Juan va a leer la Biblia todos los días.

> ~ Juan is going to read the Bible every day.

Petra va a aprender mucho de la clase.

> ~ Petra is going to learn a lot from class.

(Nosotros) vamos a vender recuerdos hechos a mano.

> ~ We are going to sell handcrafted souvenirs.

What abou a little test? Let's check your understanding of the future tense. The following sentences are in the present tense. Can you convert them to future tense statements using the IR + a + infinitive formula?

1.) *Las mujeres y me corremos el maratón juntos.* (The women and I run the marathon together.)

2.) *(Vosotros) prometeís a comportarse.* (You (boys) promise to behave.)

3.) *(Vosotras) perdeís cada año.* (You (girls) lose every year.)

4.) *(Ellos) rompen las leyes todo el tiempo.* (They break laws all the time.)

5.) *(Ustedes) creen en la biblia.* (You all) believe in the Bible.)

6.) *(Yo) escribo cartas para él.* (I write letters for him.)

7.) *(Tu) abres la puerta para mí.* (You) open the door for me.)

8.) *(Ella) describe la pintura tan bien.* (She describes the painting so well.)

9.) *(Nosotros) atendimos a los huéspedes.* (We attend to the guests.)

10.) *(Ellos) permiten mascotas dentro del hotel.* (They allow pets inside the hotel.)

11.) *El señor Domínguez conduce un coche de lujo.* (Mister Dominguez drives a fancy car.)

12.) *(Ellos) reciben pedidos por teléfono.* (They receive orders over the phone.)

13.) *(Nosotros) oímos rumores sobre ti.* (We hear rumors about you.)

14.) *El tribunal decide sobre el caso hoy en día.* (The court decides on the case today.)

15.) *(Nosotros) tenemos la piña.* (We have pineapple.)

16.) *María hace galletas.* (Maria makes cookies.)

17.) *Los estudiantes hacen la tarea.* (The students do homework.)

18.) *(Nosotros) podemos ganar el juego.* (We are able to win the game.)

19.) *(Yo) veo un avión.* (I see a plane.)

20.) *(Ellos) dicen mentiras.* (They tell lies.)

21.) *(Yo) quiero un poco de helado.* (I want some ice cream.)

22.) *(Nosotros) sabemos los hechos.* (We know the facts.)

23.) *(Ellos) conocen que la gente famosa.* (They know famous people.)

24.) *Aqui (ellos) vienen.* (Here they come.)

25.) *Mi hermana y mi salimos hoy.* (My sister and I leave today.)

26.) *(Yo) vuelvo a conocerlo.* (I return to meet you.)

27.)   *(Usted) sigue el mapa.* (You follow the map.)

28.)   *(Ellos) cuentan los turistas.* (They count the tourists.)

29.)   *(Nosotros) recordamos todo lo.* (We remember everything.)

30.)   *Los niños entienden.* (The children understand.)

QUE (THAT)

After that lengthy exercise, you should be more confident now in crafting sentences in the future tense. It's time to move on to another topic. This time we will talk about QUE which translates to English as "that." This Spanish word is a little bit more complicated. Basically, there are two uses for Que: as a relative pronoun and as a conjunction.

The Relative Pronoun *QUE*

The English language does not always use "that" as a relative pronoun. The case is different in Spanish. As a matter of fact, using *que* to refer to a previously mentioned noun is almost a requirement. The relative pronoun *que* is pretty versatile. It can be used to refer to any noun, as a subject or as an object.

Used as a relative pronoun, que means "that" but it can take on other meanings like "who," "whom" or "which." It all depends on the noun it replaces. Let's look at a few examples.

El vestido que te gusta ~ The dress that you like

Que used in place of a thing (*el vestido*) in the object position

Las cosas que vi ~ The things which I saw

Que used in place of a thing (*las cosas*) in the object position

La mujer que es amable ~ The woman who is kind

Que used in place of a person (*la mujer*) in the subject position

Las personas a las que conocí ~The people whom I met

Que used in place of persons (*las personas*) in the object position

Now let's use the phrases in complete sentences.

Estoy usando el vestido que te gusta. (I am wearing the dress that you like.)

Odio las cosas que vi. (I hate the things which I saw.)

La mujer que es amable me dio comida. (The woman who is kind gave me food.)

Las personas a las que conocí eran útiles. (The people whom I met were helpful.)

Use relative pronoun **QUE** to make sentences that are more complex. In the examples below, *Que* is used to combine 2 statements that share a common noun.

Te gusta el vestido. ~ You like the dress.

El vestido es caro. ~ The dress is expensive.

El vestido que te gusta es caro. ~ The dress that you like is expensive.

Vi cosas. ~ I saw things.

Ellos eran horribles. ~ They were horrible.

Las cosas que vi eran horribles. ~ The things which I saw were horrible.

La mujer es amable. ~ The woman is kind.

Elle me dio comida.   ~ She gave me food.

La mujer que es amable me dio comida. ~   The woman who is kind gave me food.

Me encontré con gente.   ~ I met people.

Ellos eran útiles.   ~ They were helpful.

Las personas a las que conocí eran útiles. ~ The people whom I met were helpful.

The Subordinating Conjunction *QUE*

As a subordinating conjunction, que can be used to combine two statements that may not necessarily share a common noun. The following format may be used.

main clause + ***que*** + dependent clause

Maria oído.   ~ Maria heard.

El perro se escapó.   ~ The dog escaped.

Maria oído que el perro se escapó. (Maria heard that the dog escaped.)

Lo dije antes.   ~ I said it before.

El hombre es un ladrón. ~ The man is a crook.

Lo dije antes que el hombre es un ladrón. (I said it before that the man is a crook.)

PARA (FOR)

In Spanish, the English preposition "for" has 2 equivalents: ***para*** and ***por***. Each has specific uses. We will discuss por in the succeeding chapters. For easier learning, let's focus on *para* at the moment.

1. Use ***para*** to indicate the purpose or usefulness of a thing. It can also be used to state a need or intent.

Los juguetes están hechos para los niños. (The toys are made for children.)

La copa es para el té. (The cup is for tea.)

El dinero es para ti. (The money is for you.)

2. Use ***para*** to mean "to" or "in order to." When the preposition takes on this meaning, it has to be followed by an infinitive verb.

Él trabaja para ganar dinero. (He works in order to earn money.)

Los alumnos estudian para aprender. (The students study in order to learn.)

María camina a la escuela para ahorrar dinero.
(Maria walks to school in order to save money.)

3. Use *para* to indicate or state a destination.

Señor Dominguez está viajando para una convención. (Mr. Domingues is traveling for a convention.)

La familia se marcha para Madrid mañana. (The family is leaving for Madrid tomorrow.)

4. Use *para* to indicate time or a deadline. In this case, para can be translated as "around" or "about" (the specified time or date).

Los niños van a la escuela para las seis. (The children leave for school around 6:00.)

Llegamos para el viernes. (We arrive by Friday.)

El espectáculo comienza para las diez. (The show begins at about 10:00)

5. Use *para* with the verb *estar* to talk about an event or action that is to be completed soon.

Los clientes están listos para salir. (The guests are ready to leave.)

Él está listo para volar. (He is ready to fly.)

Estamos listos para salir de la casa. (We are about to leave the house.)

6. Use **para** to indicate the recipient of a gift.

El cuadro de cholocates es para mi madre. (The box of cholocates is for my mother.)

Los juguetes son para los niños. (The toys are for the children.)

Estas flores son para ti. (These flowers are for you.)

7. Use **para** to talk about something that is unexpected.

Ella se mueve con gracia para un niño gordito. (She moves gracefully for a chubby kid.)

Eres maduro para su edad. (You are mature for your age.)

Ellos saben demasiado para un niño de diez años. (They know too much for a ten year old.)

8. Use **para** to express a personal reaction.

Es difícil para los niños. (It is difficult for the children.)

Esto no es para mí. (This is not for me.)

Se siente bien para mí. (It feels right for me.)

Por has a much longer list of uses. Knowing the uses of **para** will allow you to determine when *por* may be more appropriate to use. Don't worry though as we will get to know the other preposition in the succeeding chapters.

Chapter 9 – Adjectives and Adverbs

By now, you have learned much about adjectives as we discussed them in length in the previous chapter. There is more to learn about this subject however. And we shall start learning more now.

POSSESSIVE ADJECTIVES

There are five words that describe ownership. These are *mi, tu, su, nuestro* and *vuestro*. You can use these possessive adjectives to indicate either relationship or ownership of things. It is not however, proper to use them when referring to either body parts or pieces of clothing. Definite articles are used for that purpose. Let's look at the first three.

Mi, Tu, Su (My, Your, Their)

These possessive adjectives have two forms: singular and plural. They are not concerned about gender. You only have to focus on them agreeing with the described noun. Remember, they have to agree with the noun being described or modified and not the person or persons for that matter whom they belong to.

Singular	Plural
Mi	Mis
Mi libro	Mis libros
Mi pluma	Mis plumas

Tu	Tus
Tu guitarra	Tus guitarras
Tu perro	Tus perros
Su	Sus
Su amigo	Sus amigos
Su amiga	Sus amigas

The English equivalent of **mi** is "my." **Tu** and **Su** can be used to mean "your." While **tu** has a casual tone, **su** is used for a more formal conversation. In addition **su** can also mean "his," "her" or "their."

Mi casa es su casa. (My house is your house.)

Mi madre te gusta. (My mother likes you.)

María ama a su perro. (Maria loves her dog.)

Jorge adora a su abuela. (Jorge adores his grandmother.)

Tu madre es bella. (Your mother is beautiful.)

Sus hijos son adorables. (Their children are adorable.)

Señora Dominguez, su casa es preciosa. (Mrs. Dominguez, your house is lovely.)

Nuestro and Vuestro (Our, Your)

Both of these adjectives have four forms: singular, plural, masculine and feminine. They do not only have to agree with the quantity but also with the gender of the noun.

The English equivalent of **nuestro** is "our." Like **tu** and **su**, **vuestro** is also used to mean "your." Unlike the two however, **vuestro** is used when the possessor is more than one person. Like **tu**, its use is informal.

Masculine		Feminine	
Singular	Plural	Singular	Plural
vuestro	*vuestros*	*vuestra*	*Vuestras*
vuestro perro	*vuestros perros*	*vuestra casa*	*vuestras casas*
nuestro	*nuestros*	*nuestra*	*nuestras*
nuestro amigo	*nuestros amigos*	*nuestra amiga*	*nuestras amigas*

Maria and Jorge, vuestro perro es adorable. (Maria and Jorge, your dog is adorable.)

Maria and Jorge, que necesita para alimentar a vuestros perros. (Maria and Jorge, you need to feed your dogs.)

Vuestra casa es magnífica. (Your house is magnificent.)

¿Son todas vuestras casas así de grande? (Are all your houses this big?)

Este es nuestro amigo, Jorge. (This is our friend, Jorge.)

¿Conoce a nuestros amigos, Rodrigo y Lucas? (Have you met our friends, Rodrigo and Lucas?)

Se casó con nuestra hermana. (He married our sister.)

Nuestras hermanas llegan hoy. (Our sisters arrive today.)

DEMONSTRATIVE ADJECTIVES

In addition to their use as pronouns, "this" and "that" also serve as demonstrative adjectives.

Can I borrow this pen?

Can I borrow this?

In the first sentence "this" used as a demonstrative adjective. In the second sentence, "this" acts as a pronoun replacing "the book." As opposed to pronouns, demonstrative adjectives can answer the question "which?" Basing on the examples provided above, which pen do you want to borrow, this or that?

Spanish demonstrative adjectives behave in the same way. The difference is that the Spanish counterparts are bound by gender and quantity. And while the English "that" is typically used to point out objects at a distance, the Spanish "that" is only used to refer to objects at a short distance. For objects at a farther distance, the Spanish will say "that one over there." Let's have a look at the Spanish demonstrative adjectives.

	Masculine		Feminine	
	Singular	Plural	Singular	Plural
This/ These	*este* *este libro*	*estos* *estos libros*	*esta* *esta pluma*	*estas* *estas plumas*
That/ Those	*ese* *ese perro*	*esos* *esos perros*	*esa* *esa guitarra*	*esas* *esas guitarras*
That/ Those over there	*aquel* *aquel coche*	*aquellos* *aquellos coches*	*aquella* *aquella casa*	*aquellas* *aquellas casas*

The feminine forms of these demonstrative adjectives are only used for identified or known objects. In cases when the noun is identified or uncertain, *este*, *ese* and *aquel* are used. This rule applies to nouns that refer to an idea, a situation, a concept or an event.

WHERE DO ADJECTIVES GO? BEFORE OR AFTER NOUN?

Spanish adjectives are usually placed after the noun. From the previous lessons, however, you have been introduced to adjectives that break this rule. For instance, adjectives of quantity go before the noun instead [i.e. *pocos libros, dos perros, muchas gatos*]. There are other types of adjectives that have to be specifically placed before the noun. It's time to introduce them to you.

Adjectives of Quality

These adjectives are used to emphasize the essential qualities of nouns. What do we mean by essential quality? These are traits of a noun that may be implicitly obvious. Let's demonstrate with examples.

el valiente león ~ the brave lion

el fiel perro ~ the loyal dog

la caliente sopa ~ the hot soup

la blanca nieve ~ the white snow

el azul cielo ~ the blue sky

Adjectives That Change in Meaning

There are more flexible adjectives in a sense that they can appear before or after the noun. But their placement can affect the entire meaning of the phrase. For example, **viejo** means "old." The phrase, **mi amigo viejo** means "my elderly friend." But if you want to talk about someone you've been friends with for a long time, you should place the adjective before the noun instead. The correct phrase to use is **mi viejo amigo** which means "my longtime friend."

The general rule is this. Put the adjective after the noun for an objective description. But if you want to express an emotional meaning, you should place the adjective before the noun instead. Below is a list of adjectives that can appear either before or after the noun and how their meanings change depending on their placement.

	After Noun	Before Noun
pobre	poor/ not rich	unfortunate
simple	simple/ modest	mere
puro	pure	nothing but
triste	sad	dreadful
bueno	good/ gentle	simple
dulce	sweet	nice
sólo	lonely	one
único	unique	only
raro	strange	rare
varios	different	several

diferente/ propio	different	various
bajo	short	of low quality
alto	tall	topnotch/ high-class
grande	big	great
nuevo	newly made/ new	newly acquired/ another
antiguo	antique	old/ ancient

COMPARATIVE ADJECTIVES

Two nouns can be compared in two ways, either equally or unequally. There are specific formats for these. When making a comparison, you should always remember that the adjective should match the subject of comparison just like in this example.

Maria works as hard as Rodrigo and Jorge.

Comparison of Equality

For nouns that are similar or share a common trait, you can use this format to craft your comparative statement.

(Subject) + verb + *tan* **+ adjective +** *como*
        (as _____ as)

María trabaja tan duro como Rodrigo y Jorge. (Maria works as hard as Rodrigo and Jorge.)

Luisa lee tan rápido como Maria. (Luisa reads as fast as Maria.)

Somos tan inteligentes como los chicos. (We are as smart as the boys.)

(Tu) a tan bella como su hermana. (You are as beautiful as your sister.)

Estoy tan alto como mi hermano. (I am as tall as my brother.)

Comparison of Inequality

People, things and events are not created equal. There are points of differences. One may be inferior and the other superior. For making such a comparison, you can use the following formats.

*If the subject is more superior over the other noun, use this:

(Subject) + verb + *más* + adjective + *que*
    (more _____ than)

María trabaja más duro que Rodrigo y Jorge. (Maria works harder than Rodrigo and Jorge.)

Luisa lee más rápido que Maria. (Luisa reads faster than Maria.)

Somos más inteligentes que los chicos. (We are smarter than the boys.)

(Tu) a más bella que su hermana. (You are more beautiful than your sister.)

Estoy más alto que mi hermano. (I am taller than my brother.)

*If the subject is inferior, this format must be used.

(Subject) + verb + *menos* + adjective +*que*
(less _____ than)

Rodrigo y Jorge trabajan menos duros que Maria. (Rodrigo and Jorge works less harder than Maria.)

Maria lee menos rápido que Luisa. (Maria reads less faster than Maria.)

Los chicos son menos inteligentes que nos. (The boys are less smarter than us.)

Su hermana es menos bella que te. (Your sister is less beautiful than you.)

Mi hermano es menos alto que me. (My brother is less taller than me.)

*The inferiority of a subject may also be expressed through comparison by negation. In such a case, this format should be used.

(Subject) + *no* + verb + *tan* + adjective + *como*
(not as _____ as)

Rodrigo y Jorge no trabajan tan duros como Maria. (Rodrigo and Jorge does not work as hard as Maria.)

Maria no lee tan rápido como Luisa. (Maria does not reads as fast as Maria.)

Los chicos no son tan inteligentes como nos. (The boys are not as smart as us.)

Su hermana no es tan bella como te. (Your sister is not as beautiful as you.)

Mi hermano es menos alto que me. (My brother is less tall than me.)

SUPERLATIVE ADJECTIVES

When comparing more than two nouns with one among all being superior, we use superlative adjectives. You may want to point out the best or the worst from a bunch. In English, it is as easy as adding -est to the adjective. The Spanish however, has a different way of going about it.

Subject + verb *SER/ ESTAR* + definite article + noun + *más* (or *menos*) + adjective + *de*

This is the same way as saying, "Jorge is the tallest boy in the group." But as in English, the noun "boy" or any noun for that matter referring to the subject may also be eliminated. For instance, "Jorge is the tallest in the group." To create a sentence like this in Spanish, the following format may be used.

Subject + verb *SER/ ESTAR* + definite article + *más* (or *menos*) + adjective + *de*

Jorge es el [chico] más alto de el grupo. (Jorge is the tallest [boy] in the group.)

María es la [chica] más linda del pueblo. (Maria is the prettiest [girl] in the village.)

Este es el [lugar] más cool de la ciudad. (This is the coolest [place] in the city.)

Ellos son los [empleados] más trabajadores de la empresa. (They are the most hardworking [employees] in the company.)

María es el lector más rápido de la clase. (Maria is the fastest reader in the class.)

Son los [niños] más aplicados de la escuela. (They are the smartest [boys] in school.)

Su hermana es la más bella de su familia. (Your sister is the most beautiful in your family.)

Somos la pareja más linda de la habitación. (We are the cutest couple in the room.)

Absolute Superlative

Superlative adjectives are not only used when comparing a subject to a group. Superiority can also be expressed exclusively in relation to the main subject. In English, it is referred to as absolute superlative expression. And here are a couple of ways to do it in Spanish.

muy + adjective   i.e. *muy alto* (very tall)

sumamente + adjective   i.e. *sumamente alto* (extremely tall)

adjective + ísimo/a/os/as i.e. *altísimo* (incredibly tall)

*To use the last option, the last letter must be dropped before attaching any of the suffix. The choice of suffix to attach to the adjective must agree in gender and quantity with the noun being described or the subject in the sentence. Here are a few examples.

Maria es muy bonita. (Maria is very pretty.)

Su marido es sumamente grasa. (Your husband is extremely fat.)

Tu a guapísimo. (You are incredibly handsome.)

Sus abuelos son muy antiguos. (Your grandparents are very old.)

Estos zapatos son sumamente nueva. (These shoes are extremely new.)

El coche es rápidísimo. (The car is incredibly fast.)

Esta idea es muy estúpida. (This is a very stupid idea.)

Yo soy aburrida. (I am extremely bored.)

Estamos sanísimo. (We are incredibly healthy.)

Irregular Comparatives and Superlatives

In English, adding -er or -est to make comparative and superlatives is not applicable to all adjectives. Hence, we have words like "better," "best," "worse," "worst," etc. These are irregular adjectives and the Spanish language has them too. In other words, they do not fit in to the formats above. And there are no standard rules that govern them. That only means you have to memorize them.

Adjective	Comparative	Superlative
joven (young)	*menor que* (younger)	*el/ la menor* (the youngest)
viejo (old)	*mayor que* (older)	*el/ la mayor* (the oldest)

malo (bad)	*peor que* (worse)	*el/ la peor* (the worst)
bueno (good)	*mejor que* (better)	*el/ la mejor* (the best)

Pablo es joven. (Pablo is young.)

Pablo es menor que Juana. (The boy is younger than Juana.)

Pablo es el menor el niño de la clase. (Pablo is the youngest boy in the class.)

Eres viejo. (You are old)

Eres mayor que. (You are older than me.)

Eres el mayor entre nos. (You are the oldest among us.)

Soy una mala cantante. (I am a bad singer.)

Soy un cantante peor que él. (I am a worse singer than him.)

Soy el peor cantante nunca. (I am the worst singer ever.)

Somos buenos estudiantes. (We are good students.)

Somos mejores que ellos estudiantes. (We are better students than them.)

Somos los mejores estudiantes de la escuela. (We are the best students in school.)

Grande and *Pequeño* ("Big" and "Small")

Adjective	Comparative	Superlative
grande (big)	*mayor que* (bigger)	*el/ la mayor* (the biggest)
pequeño (small)	*menor que* (younger, less)	*el/ la menor* (the youngest, least)

These two adjectives are technically irregular but they may behave like regular verbs and follow the comparative format in some cases. When these adjectives are used in a statement referring to size, they follow the following format just like other regular adjectives.

más* (or *menos*) + adjective + *que

definite article + noun + *más* (or *menos*) + adjective + *de*

Su casa es grande. (Their house is big.)

Su casa es más grande que el nuestro. (Their house is bigger than ours.)

Su casa es más grande de el bloque. (Their house is the biggest in the block.)

Mi regalo es pequeño. (My gift is small.)

Mi regalo es más pequeño que el suyo. (My gift is smaller than yours.)

Mi regalo es más pequeño del grupo. (My gift is the smallest of the bunch.)

*However, when grande and pequeño are used to refer to age or to the idea of "greater" or "lesser" respectively, their irregular format should be used.

-ísimo/ -ísima/ -ísimos/ -ísimas

You have been introduced to the use of these suffixes to turn any adjectives into an ultimate or extreme expression. For some, its use is as simple as replacing the vowel ending of the adjective with these suffixes. But then again, it is not the same for everyone. In the irregular superlatives below, you will find that the same suffixes are attached but the adjectives go through some changes that regular superlatives don't.

Adjective	Irregular Superlative	

caliente (hot)	*calentísimo*	really hot
feliz (happy)	*felicísimo*	extremely happy
agradable (nice)	*agradabilísimo*	super nice
antiguo (old)	*antiquísimo*	very old
amargo (bitter)	*amarguísimo*	really bitter
largo (long)	*larguísimo*	very long
fresco (fresh)	*fresquísimo*	super fresh
blanco (white)	*blanquísimo*	bright white
cómico (funny)	*comiquísimo*	hilarious

Tiene una sonrisa blanquísimo. (He has a bright white smile.)

Su casa es antiquísimo. (Their house is really old.)

Estoy felicísimo. (I am extremely happy.)

Su música es fresquísimo. (Their music is super fresh.)

-bil + [-ísimo/ -ísima/ -ísimos/ -ísimas]

This rule applies to adjectives ending in **-ble**. First, drop the **-ble** ending and replace it with **-bil** before attaching **-ísimo/ -ísima/ -ísimos/ -ísimas**. A few examples include the following.

Adjective	*-bilísimo/ -bilísima/ -bilísimos/ -bilísimas*	
agradable (nice)	*agradabilísimo*	incredibly nice
amable (friendly)	*amabilísimo*	very friendly
notable (remarkable)	*notabilísimo*	extremely remarkable
miserable (miserable)	*misirabilísimo*	really miserable

Señora Dominguez es agradabla. (Mrs. Dominguez is nice.)

Señora Dominguez es agradabilísima. (Mrs. Dominguez is incredibly nice.)

Eres amable. (You are friendly.)

Eres amabilísimo. (You are very friendly.)

Los niños son notables. (The children are remarkable.)

Los niños son notabilísimo. (The children are extremely remarkable.)

Somos miserables. (We are miserable.)

Somos misirabilísimos. (We are really miserable.)

-érrimo/ -érrima/ -érrimos/ -érrimas

Instead of taking the **-ísimo/-ísima/ -ísimos/-ísimas** suffixes, many but not all qualitative adjectives that has |r| in the last syllable, adopt an -**érrimo/ -érrima/ -érrimos/ -érrimas** ending instead. The |r| and any vowel after that are dropped before adding any of the suffixes.

Adjective	-érrimo/ -érrima/ -érrimos/ -érrimas	
célebre (famous)	*celebérrimo*	super famous
libre (free)	*lebérrima*	really free
mísero	*misérrimo*	extremely

(wretched)		wretched
salubre (healthy)	*salubérrima*	very healthy

Su padre es célebre. (Her father is famous.)

Su padre es celebérrimo. (Her father is super famous.)

Este libro es libre. (This book is free.)

Este libro es lebérrima. (This book is really free.)

Son míseros criaturas. (They are wretched creatures.)

Son misérrimos criaturas. (They are extremely wretched creatures.)

Los niños y me estamos salubre. (The children and I are healthy.)

Los niños y me estamos salubérrima. (The children and I are very healthy.)

-císimo/ -císima/ -císimos/ -císimas

These suffixes are applicable to adjectives ending in -**or**, -**dor** or -**n**. In this case, no changes in the root word are necessary. You simply attach the appropriate suffix according to what the noun calls for in terms of gender and quantity.

Adjective	*-bilísimo/ -bilísima/ -bilísimos/ -bilísimas*	
inferior (lower)	*inferiorcísimo*	really low
hablador (talkative)	*habladorcísimo*	very talkative
joven (young)	*jovencísimo*	incredibly young

Su coeficiente intelectual es inferiorcísimo. (His IQ score is really low.)

Las chicas son habladorcísimo. (The girls are very talkative.)

Tu eres jovencísimo. (You are incredibly young.)

Comparison of Nouns, Verbs and Adverbs

Just like the comparison of adjectives, comparison of nouns, verbs and adverbs also follow formats depending on what is being compared and whether they are compared equally or unequally.

Equal Comparison of Quantity

Use the following format when comparing nouns or adverbs in terms of numbers or quantity. Use the appropriate form of tanto according to the noun being described. For this comparison, the conjugated form of tener ("to have") is essential.

Subject + *TENER* + tanto/tanta/tantos/tantas + noun/ adverb + como

(as many/ much _____ as...)

Tengo tantos coches como Pablo. (I have as many cars as Pablo.)

Elena tantas plumas como Maria. (Elena has as many pens as Maria.)

Tenemos tanto dinero como ellos. (We have as much as money as they.)

Tienes tanta paciencia como me. (You have as much patience as me.)

Equal Comparison of Verbs

There are basically two ways to compare verbs in a sentence.

*Use this format with the absence of adjective.

verb + tanto + como (...as much as...)

Chicken costo tanto como la carne de cerdo. (Chicken cost as much as pork.)

Él escribe tanto como Narisa. (He writes as much as Narisa.)

Las mujeres comen tanto como los hombres. (The women eat as much as the men.)

Trabajamos tanto como ellas. (We work as much as them.)

*In the following format, the adjective should always be in the masculine form. Use this with the presence of an adjective.

verb + tan + adjective (in the masculine form) + como

Coste de pollo tan alto como la carne de cerdo. (Chicken cost as high as pork.)

Él escribe tan rápido como Narisa. (He writes as fast as Narisa.)

Trabajamos tan duro como ellas. (We work as hard as them.)

Unequal Comparison of Nouns and Verbs

Follow these formats when comparing nouns and verbs. The second one indicates exact quantity in numbers.

Subject + TENER + más (or menos) + noun/ adverb + que

Subject + TENER + más (or menos) + noun/ adverb + de [for numbers]

Tengo menos coches de diez. (I have less than 10 cars.)

Tengo más coches que Pablo. (I have more cars than Pablo.)

Elena tiene menos plumas que Maria. (Elena has less pens than Maria.)

Ella tiene menos plumas de seis. (She has less than 6 pens.)

Tenemos más dinero que ellos. (We have more money than them.)

Tienes más paciencia que me. (You have more patience than me.)

Unequal Comparison of Verbs

Two people cannot do the same thing in equal degree. Use this format if you want to compare two verbs and emphasize their inequality.

verb + más/ menos + que

Chicken costo menos que la carne. (Chicken cost less than pork.)

Él escribe más que Narisa. (He writes more than Narisa.)

Las mujeres comen menos que los hombres. (The women eat less than the men.)

Trabajamos más que ellas. (We work more than them.)

Chapter 10 – Negating Statements

After our lengthy lessons on grammar, you are now well equipped to answering and asking questions, expressing yourself in the present, talking about the past and the future. But wait! You simply can't say YES to everything. This chapter will teach you how to say NO or how to create negative sentences.

The Word Is NO

Turning affirmative statements into negative ones is not as complex as you may think. As a matter of fact, all you need to do is insert a "no" in the sentence before the verb. Let us look at the examples below.

Affirmative	Negative
Soy hermosa. (I am beautiful.)	*No soy hermosa.* (I am not beautiful.)
Eres amable. (You are kind.)	*No eres amable.* (You are not kind.)
Pedro corre rápido. (Pedro runs fast.)	*Pedro no corre rápido.* (Pedro doesn't run fast.)
Estamos dejando para el Madrid. (We are leaving for Madrid.)	*No estamos dejando para el Madrid.* (We are not leaving for Madrid.)
Nos odian. (They hate us.)	*Nos no odian.* (They do not hate us.)

Does this apply to sentences in the present and future tense too? Yes they do and you will see just how in the following examples.

Affirmative	Negative
Le di el anillo de mi abuela. (I gave her my grandmother's ring.)	*Le **no di** el anillo de mi abuela.* (I did not give her my grandmother's ring.)
Tomaste mi libro. (You took my book.)	***No tomaste** mi libro.* (You did not take my book.)
Elsa llegó tarde. (Elsa arrived late.)	*Elsa **no llegó** tarde.* (Elsa did not arrive late.)
Nosotros olvidamos de la cesta de regalo. (We forgot the gift basket.)	*Nosotros **no olvidamos** de la cesta de regalo.* (We did not forget the gift basket.)
Los niños estaban bien atendidos. (The children were well behaved.)	*Los niños **no estaban** bien atendidos.* (The children were not well behaved.)
Affirmative	**Negative**
Voy a beber un vaso de leche. (I am going to drink a glass of milk.)	***No voy** a beber un vaso de leche.* (I am not drinking a glass of milk.)
Vas a comer toda la comida sobrante. (You	***No vas** a comer toda la comida sobrante.* (You

are going to eat all the leftover food.)	are not eating all the leftover food.)
Petra va a aprender. (Petra is going to learn.)	*Petra **no va** a aprender.* (Petra is not learning.)
Vamos a vender recuerdos hechos a mano. (We are going to sell handcrafted souvenirs.)	***No vamos** a vender recuerdos hechos a mano.* (We are not going to sell handcrafted souvenirs.)
Los soldados van a llegar hoy. (The soldiers are going to arrive today.)	*Los soldados **no van** a llegar hoy.* (The soldiers are not going to arrive today.)

Other Negative Words

Aside from **NO,** there are other negative words that you can use. For instance, **nunca** is the Spanish term for "never" which is the exact opposite of **siempre** which means "always." Refer to the table below for more negative words.

Affirmative	Negative
siempre (always)	*nunca* (never)
algún |-a/-o/-as/-os (something/some)	*ningún* |-a/-o/-as/-os (none, no)
algo (something)	*nada* (nothing)

alguien (somebody)	*nadie* (nobody)
también (also)	*ampoco* (not either/neither)
o...o (either...or)	*ni...ni* (neither...nor)

These negative words can stand alone. And when they are used in a sentence, they should be placed before the verb. Here are some examples.

Affirmative	Negative
Nina y María están siempre juntos. (Nina and Maria are always together.)	*Nina y María* **nunca están** *juntos.* (Nina and Maria are never together.)
Tengo algo para ti. (I have something for you.)	**Nada tengo** *para ti.* (I have nothing for you.)
Elena tiene alguna de comida para compartir. (Elena has some food to share.)	*Elena* **ningúna tiene** *de comida para compartir.* (Elena has no food to share.)
Eres alguien especial. (You are somebody special.)	**Nadie eres** *especial.* (You are nobody special.)
También queremos esto. (We also want this.)	**Ampoco queremos** *esto.* (We don't want either.)

NO + **Another Negative Word**

Although the above negative words can stand alone, they may also be combined with the word NO. In this case, NO should be placed before the verb and the other negative word should appear after the verb.

*Le **no** di el anillo de mi abuela.* (I did not give her my grandmother's ring.)

*Le **nunca** di el anillo de mi abuela.* (I never gave her my grandmother's ring.)

*Le **no** di **nunca** el anillo de mi abuela.* (I never gave her my grandmother's ring.)

***No** voy a beber un vaso de leche.* (I am not drinking a glass of milk.)

***Nada** voy a beber.* (I am drinking nothing.)

***No** voy **nada** a beber.* (I am drinking nothing.)

*A combination of negative words in a sentence is also possible. Now this may be strange to you since to negative words cancel each other out in English making the statement positive. In Spanish however, negative words should go together. It is wrong to combine NO with a positive word.

When using a combination of negative words, they should be placed next to each other after the verb unless the other negative word is NO. NO always appears before the verb. Take a look at this example.

*Jorge me **no** compra **nunca nada**.* (Jorge never buys me anything.)

PREPOSITIONS

Throughout the lessons you have come across prepositions from the examples provided. Now, we dedicate a portion of this chapter so you can also learn to use them properly. Now here is a list of the most commonly used Spanish prepositions. As you will observe from the provided examples, they usually appear after the verb.

Spanish Prepositions	Examples
a (to/at/by means of)	*Voy **a** la Iglesia.* (I am going to Church.)
con (with)	*Estás **con** Elena.* (You are with Elena.)
sin (without)	*Me voy **sin** ti.* (I am leaving without you.)
antes de (before)	*Estaba aquí **antes de** mí.* (He was here before me.)
después de (after)	*Mario va **después de** ella.* (Mario goes after her.)
en frente de (in front of)	*Ellos están **en frente de** la fila.* (They are in front of the line.)
tras	*Estamos **trás** usted.* (We are

(after/behind)	after you.)
detrás de (behind)	*Estamos* **detrás de** *usted.* (We are behind you.)
delante de (in front of)	*Estás de pie* **delante de** *él.* (You are standing in front of him.)
cerca de (near)	*La tienda está* **cerca de** *banco.* (The store is near the bank.)
fuera de (outside of)	*Esperas* **fuera de** *la habitación.* (Wait outside of the room.)
encima de (on top of)	*La caja está* **encima del** *armario.* (The box is on top of the closet.)
en (in/on)	*Ellos están* **en** *un plano.* (They are on a plane.)
dentro de (inside)	*Se esconde* **dentro del** *armario.* (He hides inside the closet.)
sobre (about/over)	*Esto es* **sobre** *mi.* (This is about me.)
bajo (under)	*Sus zapatos están* **bajo** *de la cama.* (Your shoes are under the bed.)
hacia (toward)	*Estamos corriendo* **hacia** *usted.* (We are running toward

	you.)
desde (since/from) **hasta** (until)	*Ella se quedó conmigo **desde** entonces **hasta** ahora.* (She stayed with me from then until now.)
durante (during)	*Su madre llamó **durante** la reunión.* (Your mother called during the meeting.)
entre (among/between)	*Eres el mejor **entre** el resto.* (You are the best among the rest.)
según (according to)	*Pablo está enfermo **según** usted.* (Pablo is sick according to you.)
de (of/from) - possession	*Las flores son **de** mí.* (The flowers are from me.)
contra (against)	*Las probabilidades están en **contra** de nosotros.* (The odds are against us.)

Prepositional Pronouns

From the examples above, you may have noticed pronouns that go with the prepositions. They are called prepositional pronouns. And they are the following.

Singular	Plural
mí ("me")	**nosotros/nosotras** (formal "us")
ti (casual "you")	
él (him/masculine "it")	**vosotros/vosotras** (casual "you all")
ella (her/ feminine "it")	**ellos** (masculine "them")
usted (formal "you")	
sí (yourself/himself/herself/itself)	**ellas** (feminine "them")
	ustedes (formal "you all")
	sí (yourselves/themselves)

con + mí/ti/si

When **con** appears next to **mí/ti/sí**, they are joined to form a single word.

con + mí = **conmigo** (with me)

con + ti = **contigo** (with you)

con + sí = **consigo** (with himself/ herself/ yourselves/ themselves)

Incorrect	CORRECT
Ellos se quedan <u>con mi</u>.	*Ellos se quedan*

(They are staying with me.)	*conmigo.* (They are staying with me.)
Me voy <u>con ti</u>. (I am leaving with you.)	*Me voy* **contigo**. (I am leaving with you.)
Mi hermana habla <u>con si</u>. (My sister is talking with herself.)	*Mi hermana habla* **consigo**. (My sister is talking with herself.)

*Because **consigo** is very generic, there is a helpful word that can help you determine the gender and quantity of the noun being referred to. Take a look below.

Pablo habla consigo **mismo**. (Pablo talks with himself.)

Mi madre habla consigo **misma**. (My mother talks with herself.)

Los niños hablan consigo **mismos**. (The boys are talking with themselves.)

Los niñas hablan consigo **mismas**. (The girls are talking with themselves.)

Prepositions with Nouns and Verbs

There are prepositions too, that automatically go with nouns and verbs. You will find a list of the most common ones below. When using them in a sentence, the following format should be used.

Subject + verbs + preposition + noun/pronoun

trabajar en	(to work on/at)
subir a	(to get on/get up/climb something)
sonar (o>ue) a	(to sound like something)
servir de	(to be useful as)
salir de	(to leave from/go away from somewhere)
salir con	(to date/go out with)
probar (o>ue) de **preocuparse (to worry about)**	(to try out/sample)
pensar (e>ie) en	(to think of)
pensar (e>ie) de	(to have an opinion of)
parar (se) en	(to stay in/stop at)
morirse (o>ue) de	(to die of (not literal)
morir (o>ue) de	(to die of (literally)

montar en	(to ride)
marcharse de	(to go away/leave)
gozar de	(to enjoy)
equivocarse en	(to make a mistake about)
equivocarse con	(to be mistaken about)
enojarse con	(to get angry with)
cuidar de	(to take care of something)
cuidar a	(to take care of/care for someone)
contar (o>ue) con	(to count on)
casarse con	(to marry)
asistir a	(to attend an event)
convertirse (e>ie) en	(to change into/become)
encontrarse (o>ue) con	(to run into/meet up with)
avergonzarse (o>ue) de	(to be ashamed of)

*Ella se **avergüenza de** sí misma.* (She is ashamed of herself.)

*Me **encuentro con** Pablo esta mañana.* (I am meeting up with Pablo this morning.)

*Gloria **convierte en** una mujer.* (Gloria becomes a woman.)

***Cuentamos con**tigo.* (We are counting on you.)

PREPOSITION *POR* ("FOR")

We have completed a lesson on the preposition PARA. As promised, we are dedicating a portion of the lesson for POR.

Among its many uses, the following are the most common.

   1. To state a cause or reason

In this case, POR could mean "because of."

*Llegamos tarde **por** tráfico.* (We are late because of the traffic.)

*El tráfico es peor **por** mal tiempo.* (The traffic is worse because of the bad weather.)

*Los niños están enfermos **por** esta.* (The children are sick because of this.)

   2. To state support for or action in behalf of a cause or a person

*Vamos a votar **por** usted.* (We are voting for you.)

3. To talk about an exchange

*Gracias **por** la invitación.* (Thank you for the invitation.)

4. To refer to a place

POR could mean "through" or "by."

*Son capaces de caminar a través **por** túnel.* (They will walk through a tunnel.)

*Estoy pasando **por** el mercado.* (I am passing by the market.)

5. To carry the same meaning as the English word "per"

*Ella trabaja 12 horas **por** día.* (She works 12 hours per day.)

6. To talk about someone performing an action

In this case, POR could mean "by."

*La canción es traído a usted **por** ABBA.* (The song is brought to you by ABBA.)

7. To complete certain phrases including the following

por cierto	"by the way"
por supuesto	"of course"
por lo general	"generally"
por otra parte	"on the other hand"
por fin	"finally"
por lo menos	"at least"

Conclusion

And that completes our lessons on Spanish for beginners! Thank you again for reading this book!

I hope this book was able to help you get a good grasp of the Spanish language and its intricacies.

Give yourself a tap on the shoulders. You have worked so hard learning from the smallest of words to the more complex sentences. Do not let all your hard work go to waste. Continue to practice your Spanish. Dedicate time to review the past lessons. Learn to use Spanish in your everyday conversations. Read stories written in Spanish. Watch Spanish movies. Listen to Spanish music. All these will help reinforce the language in you!

Made in the USA
San Bernardino, CA
03 September 2018